EXCHANGE RATE REGIMES
FOR EMERGING MARKETS

JOHN WILLIAMSON

EXCHANGE RATE REGIMES FOR EMERGING MARKETS
Reviving the Intermediate Option

INSTITUTE FOR INTERNATIONAL ECONOMICS
Washington, DC
September 2000

John **Williamson** has been a senior fellow at the Institute for International Economics since 1981. He was on leave as chief economist for South Asia at the World Bank during 1996–99; economics professor at Pontifica Universidade Católica do Rio de Janeiro (1978–81), University of Warwick (1970–77), Massachusetts Institute of Technology (1967, 1980), University of York (1963–68), and Princeton University (1962–63); adviser to the International Monetary Fund (1972–74); and economic consultant to the UK Treasury (1968–70). He is author or editor of numerous studies on international monetary and developing world debt issues, including *The Crawling Band as an Exchange Rate Regime* (1996), *What Role for Currency Boards?* (1995), *Estimating Equilibrium Exchange Rates* (1994), *The Political Economy of Policy Reform* (1993), *Economic Consequences of Soviet Disintegration* (1993), *Trade and Payments After Soviet Disintegration* (1992), *From Soviet Disunion to Eastern Economic Community?* with Oleh Havrylyshyn (1991), *Currency Convertibility in Eastern Europe* (1991), *Latin American Adjustment: How Much Has Happened?* (1990), and *Targets and Indicators: A Blueprint for the International Coordination of Economic Policy* with Marcus Miller (1987).

INSTITUTE FOR INTERNATIONAL ECONOMICS
11 Dupont Circle, NW
Washington, DC 20036-1207
(202) 328-9000   FAX: (202) 328-5432
http://www.iie.com

C. Fred Bergsten, *Director*
Brigitte Coulton, *Director of Publications and Web Development*
Brett Kitchen, *Director of Marketing*

Typesetting by BMWW
Printing by Kirby Lithographic, Inc.

Printed in the United States of America
02 01 00   5 4 3 2 1

Library of Congress Cataloging-in-Publication Data

Williamson, John, 1937–
    Exchange rate regimes for emerging markets : reviving the intermediate option / John Williamson.
        p. cm.
    Includes bibliographical references and index.
    ISBN 0-88132-293-8

    1. Foreign exchange—East Asia.
I. Institute for International Economics (U.S.) II. Title.
HG3976.5 .W55   2000
332.4′5′095—dc21   00-039663
                                                     CIP

The views expressed in this publication are those of the author. This publication is part of the overall program of the Institute, as endorsed by its Board of Directors, but does not necessarily reflect the views of individual members of the Board or the Advisory Committee.

Contents

Tables

Preface

There are few topics on which the International Monetary Fund, the US Treasury Department, the majority of the Meltzer Commission, and most academic economists are agreed but all have recently been claiming that the options for exchange rate policy have been hollowed out to leave a choice solely between a hard fix and a free float. Countries may fix their exchange rate with institutional arrangements to make sure it stays fixed, like a currency board or dollarization. Or they can allow their rate to float, with no more than limited management. But all these observers agree that they should not do anything in between.

This study challenges that new consensus. It charges that the conventional wisdom ignores the benefits that flow from intermediate currency regimes, and it outlines forms of an intermediate regime that would minimize the danger of crisis that has traumatized so many analysts into endorsing the extreme solutions. One might characterize these as managed flexible regimes with rules to govern the management.

The author, John Williamson, has been a senior fellow at the Institute since its founding in 1981. From 1996–99, he was on leave as chief economist of the South Asia region in the World Bank. This is his first publication for the Institute since returning to it in late 1999, and marks a return to a subject on which he made a number of contributions during his years here: *The Exchange Rate System* (1983, revised 1985), in which he developed the target zone proposal for exchange rate management; *Targets and Indicators* (1987, with Marcus Miller), which elaborated a blueprint for policy coordination among the main industrial countries; *Estimating Equilibrium Exchange Rates* (1994, editor), which suggests how such rates can be calculated in practice; and *The Crawling Band as an Exchange Rate*

Regime (1996), which demonstrated that one of the possible intermediate regimes has worked quite successfully in several emerging market economies. We hope that this new study will represent another major contribution by Dr. Williamson to the analysis of, and the creation of practical policy proposals for, effective national exchange rate systems.

The Institute for International Economics is a private nonprofit institution for the study and discussion of international economic policy. Its purpose is to analyze important issues in that area and develop and communicate practical new approaches for dealing with them. The Institute is completely nonpartisan.

The Institute is funded largely by philanthropic foundations. Major institutional grants are now being received from the William M. Keck, Jr. Foundation and the Starr Foundation. A number of other foundations and private corporations contribute to the highly diversified financial resources of the Institute. About 26 percent of the Institute's resources in our latest fiscal year were provided by contributors outside the United States, including about 11 percent from Japan. The Freeman Foundation has provided generous financial support to this project.

The Board of Directors bears overall responsibility for the Institute and gives general guidance and approval to its research program—including the identification of topics that are likely to become important over the medium run (one to three years), and which should be addressed by the Institute. The Director, working closely with the staff and outside Advisory Committee, is responsible for the development of particular projects and makes the final decision to publish an individual study.

The Institute hopes that its studies and other activities will contribute to building a stronger foundation for international economic policy around the world. We invite readers of these publications to let us know how they think we can best accomplish this objective.

C. Fred Bergsten
Director
August 2000

Acknowledgments

The author acknowledges helpful comments and feedback from two referees, from C. Fred Bergsten and other colleagues, from the participants of a study group held to discuss an early draft of the manuscript at the Institute, from seminar participants at the Korea Institute for International Economic Policy (KIEP), American University, and the IMF Asian Department, and from the participants in a conference organized by the Asian Development Bank Institute, the Centre d'Études Prospectives et d'Informations Internationales, and the KIEP in Tokyo in December 1999.

Introduction:
Challenging the New Orthodoxy

It is currently fashionable to dismiss intermediate exchange rate regimes as no longer feasible. The development of capital mobility has, it is claimed, ruled out anything other than the corner solutions—of a rigidly fixed exchange rate backed up by a currency board (or dollarization), on the one hand, or a more or less freely floating exchange rate, on the other.[1]

Other possible exchange rate regimes, such as crawling pegs, target zones, and crawling bands—as well as the adjustable peg of Bretton Woods fame, and even heavily managed floating—have supposedly been rendered inoperable by the weight of mobile capital that shifts in or out of a currency in response to expectations of exchange rate changes. The intermediate options have been hollowed out.

Among the most enthusiastic proponents of the new orthodoxy is the US Treasury Department. However, it was reported in the press that, at the inaugural meeting of the Group of Twenty countries in Berlin in December 1999, Treasury Secretary Lawrence Summers encountered strong resistance when he urged the assembled ministers to join him in ruling out International Monetary Fund (IMF) lending to countries that refuse to be polarized to one of the two approved corners. In East Asia, for example, there is a widespread fear that neither of the corner solutions would be capable of sustaining the sort of rapid growth that the region accomplished in the quarter-century before the 1997 crisis. The economies are searching for some viable intermediate option.

1. See, e.g., Crockett (1994), Eichengreen (1994), Obstfeld and Rogoff (1995), and Preeg (2000) for forceful statements of this view, and Swoboda (1986) for an early statement.

Nor is this just an eccentricity of East Asia. In a recent essay, Paul Masson (2000) makes a careful statistical examination of the way in which countries have changed their exchange rate regime over the years. He calculates a transition matrix between fixed, floating, and intermediate regimes, using two different ways of measuring which regime a country is in, and finds that the equilibrium distribution of regimes is only slightly more polarized than the current distribution. Although there has been some tendency for countries to polarize toward the extremes, it turns out that it is far weaker than one would infer from the sort of summary of Latin American experience that many economists, including myself, have been inclined to offer. For example, I said recently (Williamson 1999a, p. 3):

> A year ago, Latin America had one currency board and two floating rates among the seven major currencies. That is, three countries employed corner solutions and four were using intermediate regimes. Today there is only one left in the middle, and that is Venezuela with its old-fashioned adjustable peg, the worst of all systems. The ones that seemed to be doing something better—Brazil, Chile, and Colombia—have joined the floating currencies. The region has gone to six out of seven in extreme regimes.

The fact is, however, that many of the countries that have declared themselves to be floating do not behave that way, a phenomenon that Guillermo Calvo and Carmen Reinhart (2000) denominate "fear of floating" in a paper that documents this fact.[2]

At the 1999 Frank Graham lecture, Jeffrey Frankel (1999) laid out the reasons why "no single currency regime is right for all countries or at all times." Its argument in fact suggested that no two currency regimes exhaust the set from which countries should be expected to choose, the proposition developed in this essay.

The essay starts by examining whether the hollowing-out thesis rests on solid grounds, arguing that it contains an important element of truth but is nonetheless overdone. The corner solutions are not free of the possibility of crisis, as seems to be widely believed; more important, they also have a significant disadvantage that their apostles simply ignore. Hence, we proceed to an examination of the feasibility of modifying the familiar intermediate regimes into somewhat looser forms that would not be so vulnerable to speculative disturbances, but that might still be expected to be more conducive to sustaining competitiveness at an appropriate level and therefore to supporting rapid growth.

The essay then discusses the actions that countries can take to influence exchange rates without sacrificing domestic economic objectives, so as to make a commitment to an intermediate regime meaningful. In particular, it recommends cooperative sterilized intervention (including intervention undertaken on their own account by strong-currency countries) and a lim-

---

2. Further documentation is provided in Mussa et al. (2000, table 3.4).

ited role for price-oriented capital controls. The penultimate chapter discusses the relationship between managed floating and the intermediate regimes discussed earlier in the essay. It argues that the essential differences concern transparency and the provision of a focus that might help make speculation stabilizing. The first may explain the attractiveness of managed floating for the officials of many countries, but it also raises the question of whether the public should be as happy with this regime as many officials seem to be. Some brief concluding remarks summarize the argument and contrast the approach developed here with the standard literature.

The Crisis Problem

1

The main complaint of the critics of intermediate regimes is that they are vulnerable to speculative attack. A currency peg that has lost credibility is a standing invitation to speculators to mount a raid. A government that pegs its currency is therefore bound to assure investors that any change in the peg is unthinkable—even, or perhaps especially, when it begins to wonder whether such a change can be resisted. This inevitably means that, if and when it is forced to devalue, its own credibility will suffer. It also makes it likely that, if its assurances are believed, many of those who borrow from abroad will not bother to hedge their foreign exchange exposure. For a country with a large volume of foreign-exchange-denominated debt, this means that any substantial devaluation that may ultimately occur will pose problems of solvency to the financial and/or corporate sectors, leading to the sort of financial distress that was witnessed in East Asia in 1997 following the forced currency devaluations in the region.

As it happens, I can claim to have been one of the first economists to level this sort of critique at the adjustable peg exchange rate regime, as operated by even the major powers for the first quarter-century of the IMF's existence (Williamson 1965, 8):

> If, as seems probable, par [peg] changes tend to lead to a cumulative decrease of confidence in the future permanence of exchange rates, then the adjustable peg is unlikely to be viable indefinitely. Ever increasing destabilizing speculation will result if pegs are apt to jump; and if they lethargically sit in their holes, they will have ceased to be adjustable.

The conclusion I drew was that one needed to adopt an exchange rate regime that was less vulnerable to speculative pressures, which I contended could be provided by a crawling peg. I argued that this would enable a government to keep its exchange rate in line with the fundamentals, avoiding overvaluation developing, without offering speculators the one-way options that prompt speculative raids. In this I was obviously assuming (without articulating) the sort of "first-generation model" of exchange rate crises that was later formalized in the now-classic article of Paul Krugman (1979).

The crawling peg, along with the proposal for wider bands, was one of the principal alternative exchange rate regimes that was discussed during the international debate on limited exchange rate flexibility that took place in 1970–71 as the Bretton Woods system was breaking down. However, by 1973 the world had stumbled into a regime of laissez-faire in exchange rate policies, with most of the major currencies (and subsequently an increasing number of the minor ones as well) floating. For several years, it seemed that the only reasonable question to ask was whether there was a need for some rules to govern the way in which floating rates were managed.

By the early 1980s, however, the repeated appearance of major exchange rate misalignments among the floating currencies had led some of us to the conviction that the problem was not the way in which rates were managed, but what happened when they were not managed. It seemed that the markets displayed at best only a very weak tendency to pull exchange rates back toward any plausible concept of a medium-term equilibrium rate. Hence we began to explore the possibility of designing a more structured regime. This search resulted in the development of proposals for target zones, in recent years often called crawling bands, and ultimately to what Rudiger Dornbusch labeled "the BBC rules" (see also Dornbusch and Park 1999, 3). In this context, "BBC" stands for "band, basket, and crawl."

Before examining the content and purpose of the BBC rules, let me elaborate briefly on the rationale for having rules at all. As just stated, this is based on a concern that, in the absence of management, floating rates spend a long time away from anything that makes sense in terms of the fundamentals. Whether policy can do anything about this depends fundamentally on two issues: (1) Would it be possible to develop techniques for estimating some relevant concept of the equilibrium exchange rate, such as my "fundamental equilibrium exchange rate" (Williamson 1983, 1985, 13–16), that would command wide acceptance? (2) Are there policy variables that could be deployed to influence the exchange rate without having side effects that exceed the benefits?

So far as the first of those issues is concerned, I have endeavored to show the feasibility of making useful estimates by undertaking such calculations myself and commissioning similar exercises from others (Williamson 1985, 1994). Others have found it worthwhile to engage in similar exercises (e.g., Stein, Allen, and associates 1995; Hinkle and Montiel 1999). The IMF has been making such calculations to guide its own internal discussions at least since the European Exchange Rate Mechanism (ERM) crisis, and its retrospective assessment of the ability of its approach to identify several major misalignments indicates that, despite all the careful qualifications listed, it has found this approach useful (Isard and Mussa 1998, 19–21).

No one has any confidence that such estimates can be made at all precisely, but precision is not needed to provide useful guidance, given the size of the swings that unmanaged exchange rates have exhibited. Critics have also pointed out that fundamental equilibrium exchange rates (FEERs) are not necessarily independent of the policies that are to be used to influence the exchange rate, which is true in principle but of underwhelming quantitative significance.

The second of those issues, namely whether policy can be expected to influence the exchange rate without doing more harm than good, is treated in detail in chapter 4 below. Hence, we may now turn to considering the elements of the BBC rules.

The BBC Rules

There were four purposes in suggesting a wide band (interpreted as up to plus or minus 10 percent, or even plus or minus 15 percent). One was to make sure that the authorities did not get into the no-win situation of trying to defend a disequilibrium exchange rate, given that no one imagined it would be possible to estimate equilibrium at all precisely. A second was to permit the parity (the center of the band) to be adjusted, to keep it in line with the fundamentals, without provoking expectations of discrete exchange rate changes that might destabilize the markets. A third was to give some scope for an independent monetary policy, to be used for anticyclical purposes when a country found its cycle out of sync with the world norm.

A fourth purpose was to help a country cope with strong but temporary capital inflows. As long as a band is (even partially) credible, arbitrageurs will allow for the expected reversion of the exchange rate toward its parity, and deduct an appropriate discount from (or add an appropriate premium to) the local currency yield when they compare their expected return from moving funds in with foreign yields to decide whether to place funds in the country. Moreover, investors in the tradable goods industries may tend to look at the parity rather than the market rate when assessing whether to go ahead with potential investment projects, implying that a given deviation from equilibrium will have less effect in distorting investment decisions.

The "basket" part of the proposal suggested that economies with diversified trade would do better to peg to a basket that would roughly stabilize their effective exchange rate,[1] rather than to a single currency. At a conference in Seoul in 1996 (published as Williamson 1999b, the main part of which is reprinted as appendix 2 to this essay), I argued that there would be advantages to the East Asian currencies[2] in using a common basket of the three major world currencies (US dollar, yen, and now euro) to define their parities and thus the bands that would orient or specify their intervention policies.[3] Use of a currency basket in place of a peg to a single currency, the dollar, would tend to stabilize their effective exchange rates against capricious variations as a result of movements in third-currency exchange rates, notably the gyrations between the yen and the dollar. I showed that the economies in question would lose little in terms of stabilizing their effective exchange rates by all using the same basket (which, I argued, should be based on the direction of extra-regional trade of the region as a whole) rather than adopting different baskets based on their individual trade patterns.[4]

However, a common peg would offer the important gain of ensuring that their exchange rates vis-à-vis one another were not destabilized by shocks to the dollar-yen-euro rates, thus avoiding the possibility of inadvertent competitive devaluation, or the suspicion of deliberate competitive devaluation, as a result of different pegging policies. I argued that there was no reason why individual economies could not continue to pursue different policies as regards changes relative to their parity: Some could have a hard fix, like Hong Kong with its currency board; others might crawl against the basket, as Indonesia had been doing against the dollar; and others could use it simply as a guide to how they intervene in the foreign exchange market, as Singapore has done.

Perhaps the strongest argument for why the East Asian economies would have gained by moving to a basket peg has been made by C.H.

---

1. An "effective exchange rate" is the weighted average exchange rate against all currencies, where the weights are generally chosen to reflect the pattern of trade. (An alternative weighting system, based on trade elasticities, recognizes that countries are also important competitors, rather than just trade partners.) A "real effective exchange rate" corrects by changes in relative inflation, so that the index does not change if prices increase as much at home as the weighted average of the country's trading partners.

2. To be specific, I was thinking of the currencies of China, Hong Kong, Indonesia, Malaysia, the Philippines, Singapore, South Korea, Taiwan, and Thailand.

3. Other advocates of the use of a common basket peg by the East Asian economies include Reisen and van Trotsenburg (1988) and Ogawa and Ito (1999). Mussa et al. (2000, 59) also show some sympathy for a currency basket approach in East Asia.

4. Indonesia would have found the common basket most out of line with its individual needs, but even in this case the problem that would have been created did not seem to be serious.

Kwan (1998), who showed that the yen-dollar exchange rate had a statistically significant impact on output growth in the nine Asian economies I included in my hypothetical basket before the Asian crisis. A strengthening of the yen depreciated their real effective exchange rates, given their de facto dollar pegs, and thus accelerated their growth, whereas a weakening of the yen had the opposite effects.

Even Ronald McKinnon (2000, 58), in his paean to the East Asian dollar standard, admits that "the dollar zone was . . . buffeted by fluctuations in the yen/dollar exchange rate," and that the effect of Thailand's de facto dollar peg "was to cause Thailand's REER [real effective exchange rate] to drift upward before the currency attacks began in mid-1997." Oddly enough, McKinnon is in no way inhibited in his enthusiasm for the dollar standard by these considerations, even though the reasons he gives for advocating the dollar link—that this provided a noninflationary nominal anchor, and that it stabilized exchange rates among the East Asian currencies—would have been equally well-served by a common basket peg. Some of us will conclude instead that we would prefer to have the advantages of the dollar peg without its disadvantages, which is what a basket peg would offer.[5]

That is not to argue that every country would be well-advised to adopt a basket peg. In my study of the operation of crawling bands in Chile, Colombia, and Israel (Williamson 1996), I noted that Chile and Israel had both chosen to peg to a basket, whereas Colombia pegged to the dollar. I also argued that this was perfectly rational given the differences in their pattern of trade. Colombia's trade is dominated by the United States and other countries that peg to the dollar (like Venezuela), whereas the trade of Chile and Israel is far more diversified.

The final element of the BBC formula is the crawl. This is most often used with a view to neutralizing differential inflation. It can also be used to steer inflation down over time, as was done in Israel, although this could run the risk of undermining competitiveness if pursued too dogmatically (as happened in Russia). A crawl can also be adjusted in a fast-modernizing economy to reflect an expectation of Balassa-Samuelson productivity bias,[6] and accomplish the real appreciation that such an economy requires over time to maintain equilibrium. Finally, the rate of crawl can be changed, or occasional small parity adjustments can be superimposed on the regular crawl, to facilitate needed real adjustment.

---

5. To be fair, McKinnon advocates stabilizing the yen-dollar rate, which would also resolve the problem. But because that is unlikely to happen, the basket peg is a more relevant option.

6. See Balassa (1964) and Samuelson (1964). To reflect this factor, Chile built an annual 2 percent real appreciation into the formula for its crawl from 1995 to 1999.

Would the BBC Rules Have Avoided the East Asian Crisis?

These rules were intended to preempt the misalignments that breed speculative pressures, and thus crises, or at least crises of the character formalized in the first-generation crisis models. It is interesting to ask whether East Asia might have avoided its 1997 crisis had it been employing this type of regime. Because the crisis started with an old-fashioned balance of payments crisis explicable by a first-generation crisis model in Thailand,[7] it is natural to ask specifically whether Thailand might have averted its crisis had it been implementing the BBC rules instead of a fixed peg to a basket dominated by the dollar.

A 10 percent band would have given the baht scope to appreciate by up to 10 percent in 1994–95 when too much capital was flowing in, and the prospect of likely subsequent depreciation would presumably have deterred inflows and caused some of those who did still borrow abroad to seek cover. When circumstances changed in 1997, the baht could have depreciated by up to 10 percent from its parity, or 20 percent from its 1995 peak. In addition, a basket (created, let us suppose, to replicate the actual baht rate in 1994) would have lopped some 5 percent off the effective depreciation of 1995 and some 3 percent off the effective appreciation of 1997, and might also have encouraged covering of dollar-denominated borrowing. A downward crawl of, say, 3 percent per year initiated in 1994 would also have added to the expected cost of, and thus deterred, foreign borrowing—as well as leading to a 9-percent depreciation by 1997.

In sum, the baht could have been up to 12 percent stronger in 1995, thus limiting the boom, and up to 22 percent weaker in 1997, without breaking the rules of the system. That might well have been enough to remove the incentive for the speculative attacks that initiated the crisis. Admittedly, this would have been unlikely to avoid rather than merely postpone the crisis if inflows of uncovered short-term dollar-denominated debt had remained the same, but the regime would also have been helpful in deterring these inflows and encouraging borrowers to cover. In short, it is entirely possible that a well-managed BBC regime in Thailand would have avoided the East Asian crisis entirely.

Unfortunately, one cannot make an equally convincing case that a BBC regime could have saved other victims of the crisis from contagion once

---

7. Weaknesses in the Thai financial system had surfaced even before 2 July 1997, but these would have been easily manageable in the absence of the disastrous impact on balance sheets of the baht devaluation, especially in view of Thailand's low public debt and fiscal deficit. The main significance of those weaknesses in terms of precipitating the crisis was to make speculators doubt the willingness of the Thai authorities to raise interest rates in defense of the baht.

Thailand had succumbed. The Indonesian experience is particularly telling. Indonesia had been operating a de facto crawl for some years and was gradually widening its band before 1997. It responded to the Thai devaluation that initiated the East Asian crisis in July 1997 by widening its band from 8 to 12 percent. The rupiah depreciated by 8 percent, toward the weak edge of the band, in the next 10 days, and then remained within the band for another month until contagion suddenly hit, whereupon the band was abandoned with hardly a fight.

The subsequent depreciation of the rupiah was the immediate cause of the financial distress that Indonesia suffered, because many corporations had borrowed in dollars, failed to hedge, and found themselves unable to maintain debt service when their rupiah obligations exploded. Note that Indonesia's macroeconomic policies, including its exchange rate policy,[8] were given good marks by most economists right up to the crisis, even after Thailand had succumbed. One might even wonder whether Indonesia should not have attempted to defend its band instead of abandoning it without a fight, because once the band went there was a scramble to cover exposed foreign exchange positions that simply intensified the depreciation and ensured total collapse. I have to admit, however, that most of those who were closely in touch with events in Indonesia are convinced that any such attempt would have been doomed to failure, and I have no way of proving them wrong. If that is so, it implies that even good exchange rate management using the BBC rules is not proof against strong contagion effects, which Morris Goldstein, Graciela Kaminsky, and Carmen Reinhart (2000) show to have been the origin of the Indonesian crisis.

Stanley Fischer (1999) has pointed to Mexico, South Africa, and Turkey as countries that adopted floating rates and might have been expected to succumb to contagion, but did not. The contrast between their experience in escaping the worst of the crisis and that of Indonesia suggests that the weakness of the BBC regime is its vulnerability to contagion. When the markets panic, simply having a band can create a problem.

This is a significant modification of the conclusions I reached in Williamson (1996), where I reviewed the operation of crawling bands in Chile, Colombia, and Israel, the three countries that had operated the BBC rules in a fairly systematic way for at least 3 years before 1995–96. I chron-

---

8. My one criticism was that it used the dollar rather than a basket as a peg. This had led it, along with the rest of East Asia, to an unwanted appreciation of the effective exchange rate as a by-product of the yen's depreciation against the dollar after the middle of 1995. But I see little evidence that the rupiah was overvalued. Exports were still growing rapidly, at a rate of 9.0 percent in 1996 and 7.9 percent in 1997. The current account deficit peaked at 3.6 percent of GDP in 1995 and 3.4 percent of GDP in 1996, which is about the maximum that can be considered prudent but was not grossly excessive in the way that Thailand's deficit was. Growth remained strong. Goldstein, Kaminsky, and Reinhart (2000) find few of their crisis indicators to have been signaling an Indonesian crisis before the Thai crisis.

icled the history of each of the three countries after they adopted a crawling band, used their experiences to assess the viability of the crawling band as an exchange rate regime, and endeavored to compare their fortunes with those of countries that had employed alternative regimes.

I concluded (1996, 101) that the evidence "suffices to dismiss any claim that the success of countries that have employed crawling bands is simply a reflection of the strength of their fundamentals. It also surely lays to rest once and for all the charge that a crawl precludes a reduction in inflation. Indeed, it suggests that a crawling band is capable of achieving a reasonable trade-off between the conflicting objectives of reducing inflation and maintaining export growth." I also argued (1996, 79): "It seems clear that the lesson drawn from the collapse of the narrow-band Exchange Rate Mechanism in Europe [regarding the infeasibility of all intermediate regimes] . . . is wrong: a system of crawling bands can still provide a viable intermediate exchange rate regime."

More than 3 years and many more crises later, it would be fatuous to argue that history has confirmed the optimistic tone of those conclusions. First and foremost, disaster befell Indonesia because of contagion. The other unhappy experience occurred in Russia, which had used a crawling band after 1995 to limit exchange rate volatility and bring its inflation under control, which it actually succeeded in doing. But, unfortunately, Russia made the same error that Mexico had in the years that led up to the tequila crisis and that Brazil made in the run-up to its 1999 crisis: They all tried to use a crawling exchange rate as a hard nominal anchor, and became seriously overvalued as a result. Crises explicable by first-generation models were in each case the predictable consequence. All three countries reacted to their crises by allowing their exchange rates to float (even if they do not all pass the Calvo-Reinhart tests for being fearless floaters; see appendix 1).

But neither contagion nor failure to manage crawling bands properly is capable of explaining other cases in which countries have abandoned what looked like rather successful crawling bands. In particular, both Chile and Colombia abandoned their crawling bands in September 1999 and let their currencies float. The Chilean peso depreciated about 6 percent, to close to the edge of its former band, while interest rates edged up. It is not clear what is supposed to have been gained by this exercise, but so far there is no obvious cost either.

Colombia abandoned its band not because of dissatisfaction with the way that it was working but because the intellectual fad for floating had infected Wall Street to the point where simply having a band was leading to suspicions that the authorities had something to hide. Neither the exchange rate nor the interest rate changed significantly after the band was abandoned, confirming that the authorities did this because the band had lost credibility with the market rather than because it was constraining them from making some desired policy change. Israel has gradually widened its band (to a current width of about 30 percent[9]) to a point where its currency is now close to floating; at least, there is no relevant limit to it weakening. Much the same is happening in Poland, which started crawling in 1991, had a fairly wide band by 1995, and has subsequently widened it three times to a point where it is now plus or minus 15 percent.

Thus it seems that most of the countries that have abandoned crawling bands were not so much forced to do so by the pressures of crisis as seduced by the charms of floating or pressured by intellectual fashion. It does not follow that they plan to practice "fearless floating," previously known as "clean" floating; one may speculate that it is more likely that they will enter the ranks of the managed floaters. We will reserve for chapter 5 a discussion of what it is about managed floating that gives it its charm, to both policymakers and many academic economists.

A final element of the critique of intermediate regimes is provided by the second-generation models of balance of payments crises. These models, pioneered by Obstfeld (1986), show how a crisis can result from self-fulfilling expectations. An equilibrium may be perfectly viable in the absence of a speculative attack; nevertheless, if such an attack occurs, it may be rational or even inevitable for the authorities to modify their policies in a way that ratifies the attack and allows the speculators to profit from it.

A recent twist is that this can occur only if there is some preexisting weakness in the fundamentals, such as the high level of unemployment in Europe in 1992 or the vulnerable banking systems in East Asia in 1997, although one that is not so serious as to make a crisis inevitable (Wyplosz 1998). Even those of us who were initially skeptical of these models find that this modified version provides a more convincing explanation of the ERM crises of the early 1990s or the contagion that laid East Asia low than do the first-generation models.

---

9. Israel has abolished the concept of a central rate or parity, so it is no longer appropriate to describe its band as plus or minus 15 percent.

2

The End of Intermediate Regimes?

The previous chapter conceded that even a well-managed BBC regime appears to be vulnerable to contagion. The second-generation crisis models suggest why countries may become victims of contagion, even if the fundamentals would have been perfectly consistent with continued good performance in the absence of an attack. Moreover, the BBC rules require a certain sophistication in the conduct of macroeconomic policy that is not always evident. Does it follow from this critique that attempts to operate intermediate exchange rate regimes should be abandoned?

Note first that the critique does not apply to all countries (Masson, Jadresic, and Mauro 1999). There are still a number of countries, most of them distinctly low-income, which are effectively isolated from the international capital market, and which therefore could continue to operate an intermediate regime, possibly including an adjustable peg (although even such countries need to be concerned about the danger of promoting capital flight). The critique is intended to apply only to countries with a high degree of capital mobility, which means the industrial countries and the emerging markets.

Are the Corners Crisis-Proof?

More important, the impression left by this type of critique is that crises will be eliminated by moving to one of the corners. This is too strong. So far, the record of both corners in this respect has been quite good; no currency board has ever been abandoned under the pressure of a speculative crisis, and no economy that had been allowing its currency to float reasonably freely has suffered a crisis anywhere near as acute as those experienced by the East Asian victims of the 1997 crisis. But one must not conclude from this that such crises are impossible.

Consider first the case of a currency board. These have already been subjected to substantial speculative pressure, both in Argentina in 1995 and 1998, and in Hong Kong in 1997 and 1998. The attack on the Hong Kong dollar in October 1997 was traumatic, with interest rates rising for a short time to about 280 percent and the stock market falling by 10.4 percent (resulting in a 2.3 percent decline in the Dow Jones Industrial Average in New York later that day). It appears that these severe effects were due to specific design flaws in the Hong Kong system, notably the microscopic size of the monetary base (Chan 1999), which have subsequently been corrected in a way that makes the Hong Kong Monetary Authority operate more like a classical currency board.[1]

Nevertheless, the same potential weakness remains in the Hong Kong system as in every other currency board: Foreign exchange reserves are not enough to cover all of M3, and therefore they are not large enough to cover all potential demands in the event of a catastrophic loss of confidence that results in capital flight. The currency board rule is that foreign reserves should cover all of M0, which is normally substantially less than M3. Because a failure to convert M3 into M0 on demand would constitute a monetary crisis even more severe than a failure to convert M0 on demand into dollars, it is wrong to believe that a foreign reserve at least the size of M0 makes a crisis impossible.

So far, such a crisis has not happened. Currency boards have allowed a run on the currency to raise interest rates, which provides an automatic stabilizing feedback that discourages further withdrawals. But that mechanism works only as long as the public has confidence that the exchange rate will be sustained. If and when some currency board is overwhelmed, as Argentina presumably feared was about to happen when it started talking of dollarization in 1998, the confidence that has so far underpinned currency boards will evaporate overnight. If that ever happens, it is not clear that currency boards will be much more stable than any other form of

---

1. The difficulty of intervening in the foreign exchange market led the Hong Kong government to intervene in the stock market instead during the subsequent speculative attack in August 1998. It spent some HK$120 billion buying up something like 10 percent of the stocks in the Hang Seng index, to the great indignation of those (such as the editorial writers of the *Wall Street Journal*) dedicated to keeping the world safe for speculators—no matter how dangerous this makes it for the rest of us. This defeated the so-called double play, in which speculators had first sold the Hang Seng index short and then sold the Hong Kong dollar, which they reckoned would force interest rates up and therefore force stock prices down, so that they would make a profit whether or not the Hong Kong dollar was devalued. The government is reported to have sold some HK$30 billion worth of the stocks so far, when the Hang Seng index was trading at about 13,000, compared with about 7,700 when it bought the stocks—i.e., with a good profit to the Hong Kong taxpayers.

pegged exchange rate in which the central bank plays by the gold standard rules of the game by tightening monetary policy when reserves decline.

The sort of crisis that could arise with floating exchange rates is similar to that which actually occurred in East Asia in 1997. It was, after all, the collapse of those currencies after they were set free to float that generated the balance sheet problems that made the crisis so severe. The claim made for floating is that borrowers would not make the mistake of failing to hedge if they were not being tempted into imprudence by official assurances that the exchange rate is effectively fixed. But if they ever did become equally exposed, and the exchange rate subsequently collapsed, the consequences would be as severe as they were in East Asia in 1997. This is less likely, inasmuch as borrowers will witness continual fluctuations that will caution them against accepting foreign exchange exposure, but it would be complacent to deny the possibility that one day the markets could come to believe that economy X has entered a new era which provides assurance that its markets and its currency can only rise. (If such things can happen in the New York stock market,[2] they can surely happen in emerging markets.) Once again, therefore, we cannot rule out the possibility that a corner solution may permit a crisis to develop.

The Positive Side of Intermediate Regimes

That crises are not completely ruled out by the corner solutions hardly makes a compelling case for an intermediate regime, for I have already conceded that crises appear to be more probable under even well-managed intermediate regimes. Any case for an intermediate regime has to be based on an argument that they are capable of performing better than either of the corner solutions in some other important way. The natural claim is that they are better at doing what they are designed to do, which is to avoid misalignments without a major sacrifice of domestic economic objectives.

To those with sufficient ideological faith that free markets always know best, it is inconceivable that the market could, of its own accord, generate anything that could legitimately be called a misalignment. But almost everyone agrees that we have in fact witnessed repeated misalignments since the start of floating exchange rates in 1973, and it really does require faith to explain these away as a consequence of misguided policies rather than market failure. For example, everyone currently (as of 29 February 2000) seems to agree that the euro is greatly undervalued, and yet no one can explain on which side of the Atlantic macroeconomic policy is so far adrift as to provide a plausible explanation. The alternative view is that there is no particular reason why the euro should yesterday have been

---

2. See Shiller (2000), whose analysis is in many ways parallel to mine.

worth $0.96 rather than, say, $1.46; in the absence of any official attempt to limit misalignments, random market processes just happened to carry it there. Similar misalignments have recurred repeatedly since the advent of floating. For example, the US dollar went from being chronically overvalued in the mid-1980s, to ridiculously undervalued in early 1995, to overvalued again in early 2000. The yen has been a large part of the obverse side of that roller coaster, with the euro's present undervaluation another (and currently more important) part of the obverse. The pound sterling has experienced periodic overvaluations, most acutely in the early and late 1980s, and again in the spring of 2000. All the East Asian currencies went through a period of acute undervaluation shortly after starting to float. For a time, one told oneself that the industrial-country misalignments were an infant-market phenomenon (just as people have recently been explaining away the initial collapse of the East Asian currencies), and that the market would learn so that such errors would not recur. But, so far, this hope has proved unjustified. The evidence now suggests that periodic large misalignments are simply a fact of life under floating rates.

There is, of course, another corner solution besides free floating—namely, a truly fixed exchange rate, with the institutional arrangements to keep it fixed. But this does not guarantee an absence of misalignments either. More (or, in principle, less) inflation than that in the country whose currency is being used as a peg can lead to progressive emergence of overvaluation (or undervaluation), which has been a frequent cause of crises. Argentina is a conspicuous current case of a country that is paying the price of overvaluation to maintain its currency board, and is therefore saddled with an intractable problem of unemployment. Real shocks, such as large permanent changes in the terms of trade or in capital flows, can also lead to misalignments under permanently fixed exchange rates.

Misalignments, defined as large and prolonged departures from what I termed the "fundamental equilibrium exchange rate" (Williamson 1985, 13–14), can have serious consequences for the economy. Large undervaluations can have all the ill effects that were so dramatically evident in East Asia (most conspicuously in Indonesia) in late 1997 and early 1998, notably the impact on financial solvency, and hence the deflationary consequences, of an increased real value of the foreign currency debt, and the inflationary effects of high import and export prices in domestic currency.[3] And large overvaluations can lead to either unemployment or a buildup of foreign debt and an erosion of the incentive to invest in the tradable goods industries—which may make it progressively more difficult and costly to adjust the balance of payments when the need arises, or may make growth dangerously lopsided, or may slow down growth entirely.

---

3. There is no paradox in saying that devaluation can be both deflationary and inflationary. It is perfectly possible, indeed it is normal, for an exchange rate depreciation to have simultaneously a deflationary effect on output and an inflationary effect on prices.

A Historical Comparison: India and New Zealand

Let me use a particular historical comparison to make the case that misalignments can be of considerable significance in determining economic performance. Consider the experience of India, which was one of the more sclerotic developing economies before an extensive, if still very incomplete, liberalization program was initiated in 1991. India undertook its microeconomic reforms in the midst of a balance of payments crisis that required a fiscal correction, which started off quite strongly but soon petered out. It had a (heavily) managed floating exchange rate and a pragmatic monetary policy, which reacted strongly only when inflation went above 10 percent. The capital account was heavily controlled, although there was some gradual liberalization, especially on the inflow side, in the course of the 1990s. Reserves were built up from $1.1 billion in the middle of 1991 to $27.3 billion at the end of 1998, through repeated intervention in the foreign exchange market when conditions permitted.

India suffered 1 year of recession in 1991–92, before bouncing back to near its previous trend rate of growth (5.3 percent in 1992–93), and then accelerating in the mid-1990s to achieve 3 consecutive years of growth of more than 7 percent. During the 7 years following the start of the microeconomic reforms, its average growth rate was 0.5 percent above its average trend growth of 5.9 percent during the 10 years before reform, while its ratio of foreign debt to GDP decreased from 36 percent in 1991 to 24 percent in 1998. As most economists would expect, India reaped a bonus from implementing liberalizing microeconomic reforms, and without any inordinate delay.

Contrast this experience with that of New Zealand, which was probably the most sclerotic of the economies belonging to the Organization for Economic Cooperation and Development (OECD) in 1984, when it initiated a much-needed, very thorough liberalization of its economy. Its microeconomic reforms were accompanied by a policy of free floating of the exchange rate, monetary tightening, a rather slow restoration of fiscal discipline, and removal of all controls on capital inflows. Before long, the combination of reforms that excited Wall Street and a lopsided macroeconomic policy mix prompted a capital inflow and a large appreciation of the nominal and therefore the real exchange rate, and hence induced a large current account deficit and a slowdown in growth. In fact, per capita income stagnated for 8 years after the initiation of reform, while unemployment rose from 2 to 11 percent, income distribution became noticeably more unequal, and the foreign debt built up to more than 80 percent of GDP.

Only in 1992 did New Zealand's inflation fall to the range of less than 2 percent, which had been mandated as the unique objective of the central bank, and thus permit an easing of monetary policy, which brought the exchange rate back to a realistic level that permitted a resumption of growth. In the 7 years following the initiation of microeconomic liberalization, the growth rate averaged only 0.3 percent, a full 2 percent less than the average 2.3 percent growth during the 10 years before the initiation of reform. Although growth benefits did eventually come through, in the 1990s, they were awfully slow in appearing.

What can explain this striking contrast between the way in which India rather promptly began securing the growth acceleration that most of us would expect a process of microeconomic liberalization to bring, versus the long delay before New Zealand began reaping any benefits? The obvious explanation is in their very differing macroeconomic policy stances, of which their differing exchange rate policies were an integral part. India managed the exchange rate with an objective, inter alia, of maintaining competitiveness, and it chose a policy of accumulating reserves, a fiscal-monetary mix, and controls on capital inflows that were all reasonably consistent with that objective. New Zealand made no attempt to restrain the upward float of the exchange rate—not by intervening to accumulate reserves, not by seeking a fiscal-monetary mix consistent with maintaining competitiveness, not by seeking to limit the capital inflow attracted by an ideological stance congenial to Wall Street, not even by jawboning. Perhaps there is a better explanation of the sharply differing experiences of India and New Zealand after both moved to liberalize sclerotic economies, but I cannot figure what it might be.[4]

Avoiding Misalignments

I would conjecture that New Zealand's disappointing growth experience under floating rates, despite its bold reforms, is not an accident. One of the factors that appears on almost everyone's list of explanations of the East Asian miracle was the policy in that region of maintaining competitive exchange rates. I worry that it will be impossible to replicate the sort of sustained boom experienced by East Asia in the quarter-century before the crisis under the policy du jour of reasonably free floating of the exchange rate combined with a liberal capital account, and I believe that it is indeed this concern that underlies the widespread "fear of floating" in East Asia.

Imagine a country that gets its policies in good order so that it would be capable of achieving rapid growth. It will quickly be discovered by

---

4. A common but surely misguided reaction is to dismiss any comparison between India and New Zealand on the ground that India is a much poorer country with a potential for catch-up growth that is lacking in New Zealand. I have allowed for this in my comparison by contrasting the change in the growth rate pre- versus post-liberalization in the two countries, rather than contrasting India's post-liberalization 6.4 percent growth with New Zealand's 0.3 percent. It is surely time we dismissed the idea that it is per se illegitimate to compare a developing with an industrial country. For a broadly similar interpretation of the New Zealand experience to mine, see Reisen and Journard (1992).

Wall Street and deluged by vast capital inflows, which will push the domestic currency up and undermine the competitiveness of its tradable goods industries—as happened in New Zealand—thus either discouraging investment overall and bringing the boom to a quick halt, or else redirecting investment toward the nontradable goods industries and making the boom so lopsided that it will expire in a balance of payments crisis after a somewhat longer period. In this view, a period of sustained high growth will require an attempt to maintain a competitive exchange rate, by means of some combination of intervention, manipulation of the fiscal-monetary mix, controls on capital inflows, and so on.

Is there any evidence in recent experience that might confirm or refute this conjecture? Consider table 2.1, which shows all the instances since 1980 in which economies with a population of more than 5 million have achieved an annual GDP growth rate of more than 6 percent and sustained that rate for at least 3 years, and names their exchange-rate regimes at the time. There were 33 such instances of rapid growth. Some, such as Angola, Mozambique, and Rwanda, can doubtless be explained as recoveries from civil conflict rather than a reflection of successful economic policies, but no attempt has been made to exclude such cases of dubious relevance from the sample. Of these cases, 17 out of 33 had de jure or de facto pegged exchange rates. Two, (Argentina and Hong Kong) had a hard fixed exchange rate backed up by a currency board. Two (Chile, 1987–89, and Indonesia) had crawling pegs, and 3 (Chile, 1991–93 and 1995–97, and Poland) had crawling bands. That left 9 cases of floating rates, of which in at least 7 (India, South Korea, 1981–89 and 1994–96; Malaysia; Taiwan, 1986–89 and 1991–95; and Turkey) the rate was heavily managed. The only 2 cases of economies with a reasonably freely floating exchange rate achieving rapid growth were Peru in 1995-97 and Uganda in 1993–96. (The Calvo-Reinhart tests actually suggest that even these are questionable cases of free floating, see appendix 1.)

The Peruvian case is instructive. In the mid-1990s, there was much talk in the financial markets about how Peru was set to achieve years of rapid growth, but in fact this was not sustained in the way that it was in its neighbor Chile. The Chileans had indeed been motivated in their choice of exchange rate policy by the fear of exactly what happened to Peru, namely, an attack of Dutch disease induced by excessive capital inflows. So we have to rely on the Ugandan case to provide a counterexample to my conjecture. Obviously this evidence is not compelling, but it is surely enough to suggest that there may be a problem.

The major objective of adopting a crawling band is to forestall the emergence of misalignments, or at least to limit their size. The first reason for expecting it to have that effect is that it frees policy to pursue that objective: The authorities are under no obligation to defend a rate constant when changing circumstances mean that the equilibrium rate has changed, nor to turn a blind eye when a floating rate loses touch with the

Table 2.1   Cases of economies with fast growth since 1980

Country	Period	Average	Exchange rate regime
Angola	1995–97	10.2	Pegged
Argentina	1991–94	8.5	Currency board
Cameroon	1981–86	9.0	Pegged
Chile	1987–89	8.2	Crawling peg
	1991–93	9.1	Crawling band
	1995–97	8.4	Crawling band
China	1982–88	11.3	De facto peg
	1991–97	11.2	De facto peg
Egypt	1982–85	7.5	Pegged
El Salvador	1992–95	6.8	Pegged
Hong Kong	1986–88	10.7	Currency board
India	1994–96	7.6	Managed float
Indonesia	1988–96	7.9	Crawling peg
Malaysia	1988–97	8.8	Managed float
Mozambique	1987–89	9.8	Pegged
Myanmar	1992–96	7.3	Pegged
Nigeria	1988–91	8.4	Pegged
Pakistan	1980–83	7.9	Pegged
Peru	1993–95	9.0	Float
Poland	1995–97	6.7	Crawling band
Rwanda	1995–97	19.8	Pegged
Slovak Republic	1995–97	6.7	Pegged
South Korea	1981–89	9.1	Managed float
	1994–96	8.2	Managed float
Syria	1990–95	7.5	Pegged
Taiwan	1986–89	10.1	Managed float
	1991–95	6.6	Managed float
Thailand	1987–95	9.9	Pegged
Turkey	1995–97	7.3	Managed float
Uganda	1988–90	7.0	Pegged
	1993–96	8.9	Float
Venezuela	1990–92	7.4	Pegged
Vietnam	1991–97	8.4	Pegged

Notes: Fast growth is defined here as an annual GDP growth rate of more than 6 percent sustained for at least 3 years. The economies considered have populations of at least 5 million.

Source: World Bank Database.

fundamentals. They can take policy actions designed to limit misalignments. For this reason alone, it is to be expected that a crawling band or other intermediate regime will do better than either of the corners in avoiding misalignments.

But there is a second reason, too, first formalized in Paul Krugman's (1991) classic paper on target zones. His model suggests that the expectation of intervention at the margin should make speculators act in a stabilizing way. In some ways, the evidence has not been kind to this model; for example, exchange rates in band systems do not spend most of their time close to the edge of the band, as his model predicts (Svensson 1992, 128).[5] A possible explanation for this is that authorities intervene within bands as well as at the margins. This suggests that a more appropriate test of the efficacy of bands is whether they are effective in inducing mean-reverting behavior by market participants.

The evidence shows that, under a floating exchange rate, a change in the spot exchange rate is normally associated with an almost identical change in the forward rate (Svensson 1992, 132), signifying that there is a virtually complete lack of any market expectation that the exchange rate will revert toward an equilibrium level within any time horizon relevant to market participants. Matters are very different in the presence of an exchange rate band. Although bands do not normally have full credibility, and sometimes lack any credibility at all, the evidence shows that, when a rate moves within a band, the forward rate normally changes by less than the spot rate, indicating that the market expects that the spot rate will tend to revert toward the center of the band (Svensson 1992, 132–33). The obvious explanation is that, except where it has become clearly unrealistic, a band performs the function of crystallizing market expectations of where the equilibrium rate lies, and thus makes expectations stabilizing at the time horizons relevant for influencing market behavior. This is the fundamental reason for preferring a band system rather than allowing the exchange rate to float.

Nowadays many officials appear to believe the exact opposite of the Krugman logic. Edges to bands are alleged to provide the market with targets to attack, rather than assuring the market that the rate will not move further. One reason that might make sense of this is that on altogether too many occasions, authorities have attempted to defend rates that were misaligned, which allows a clear speculative profit from a successful attack. It is important to understand that traditional theory implies that a "successful" attack on a correctly aligned band cannot be expected to bring profit to the speculators collectively (e.g. a rate that is pushed to an

---

5. However, Schulstad and Serrat (1995) have argued that the conventional bilateral model of a target zone is a poor way to model the ERM. Their multilateral model of a target zone appears to fit the ERM data much better, without any need to invoke intramarginal intervention.

undervalued level by a speculative attack will result in a surplus on non-speculative transactions, so that the rate would return to the band if the speculators tried collectively to move back into the currency they had sold so as to realize their paper gains). Second-generation crisis models imply that a well-aligned band might become misaligned as a consequence of the attack itself, and thus make more sense of the view that bands provide targets to attack.

The empirical evidence nonetheless suggests that the Krugman model is closer to the truth than the view that bands are destabilizing. The strongest evidence to that effect is that of Andrew Rose (1996), who has shown that a band has a pronounced effect in limiting exchange rate variability. Indeed, he argued that the primary difference between exchange rate regimes lies not in macroeconomic fundamentals, whether one might wish to interpret these as cause or consequence of the regime, but in the noisiness of the exchange rate. He showed that this is not because some other variable, such as the interest rate, jumps around much more to keep the exchange rate stable with a band to limit variability; on the contrary, the increased exchange rate stability is essentially a free good.

In a subsequent paper, Olivier Jeanne and Andrew Rose (1999) try to explain these stylized facts by the way in which a floating exchange rate attracts noise traders, who manage to make money out of introducing noise into the exchange market. (The most plausible theory of where these profits come from is that of Krugman and Miller (1993), who postulate that they come from stop-loss traders, who essentially buy insurance against big exchange rate movements.) If the authorities pursue policies that suppress the volatility, the noise traders will find life uninteresting and go elsewhere in search of greener pastures—noisier markets.

No one is likely to mistake this for a complete theory of the foreign exchange market. But the question is whether it does not capture an important aspect of reality that is neglected by conventional macroeconomic analyses of exchange rates, which postulate that these are always pinned down by rational expectations to levels dictated by the fundamentals. Insofar as one believes that noise traders really exist, and that they can and do push exchange rates to misaligned levels that have damaging macroeconomic consequences, one will conclude there is scope for well-conceived exchange rate policy to produce better outcomes than unmanaged floating. The next question to which we need to turn is what policy might merit the appellation "well-conceived," in a world where contagion can wreak havoc with even a well-managed crawling band.

3

Can Intermediate Regimes Be Crisis-Proofed?

Are there ways in which "formal" intermediate regimes (as opposed to managed floating, which is discussed in chapter 5) might be made less vulnerable to crisis? I will focus attention initially on how vulnerability to crisis might be reduced. It is also important to consider whether this could be done without losing the ability to focus expectations (of both the authorities and the private sector) on exchange rates in the vicinity of long-run equilibrium, so as to help curb misalignments. But I will leave till later the task of asking whether the regimes discussed would still be capable of performing that function.

Of the three features of the BBC regime, it is the existence of a band—rather than the use of a basket to insulate the effective exchange rate against the vagaries of the yen-dollar-euro cross-rates or the use of a crawl to neutralize differential inflation—that makes intermediate regimes potentially crisis-prone. As pointed out above, had the East Asian currencies been pegging to a basket in the period 1995–97, it would have been mildly helpful in avoiding their effective depreciation in 1995 and the subsequent effective appreciation. The differences would not have been dramatic, but they would have gone in the right direction. Similarly, Indonesia would clearly have been in a hopeless position without its crawl. It is the obligation to intervene at the edge of a conventional band, to prevent the market rate moving outside the band, which can trigger a crisis. Thus it is modifying the obligation to intervene at the edge of the band that needs to be examined. Three possibilities merit discussion: reference rates, soft margins, and monitoring bands.

The Reference Rate Proposal

Shortly after the advent of generalized floating in 1973, it was suggested by Ethier and Bloomfield (1975) that the authorities of countries with floating exchange rates should undertake a commitment not to push their currencies away from an agreed-on estimate of the equilibrium exchange rate. The concept of an equilibrium exchange rate that they had in mind was pretty much the same as that which I subsequently termed the "fundamental equilibrium exchange rate" (Williamson 1985, 13–16), and it is this which they called the "reference rate." The authorities would have no obligation to intervene to defend that rate, but simply would be required to avoid intervening, or conducting other policies intended to influence the exchange rate, in a way that would push the market rate away from this reference rate.

The Guidelines for Floating adopted by the IMF in 1974 had actually included reference to "some target zone of rates . . . within the range of reasonable estimates of the medium-term norm," and legitimized aggressive intervention to push the rate toward such a zone provided it had been endorsed by the IMF. But in the mid-1970s the US Treasury was run by ideological floaters who thought it wrong for governments to try and think where exchange rates ought to be, and so the reference rate proposal got dismissed from discussion, along with the target zones of the Guidelines, when the Second Amendment to the IMF's Articles blessed laissez-faire in exchange rate policy.

It is obvious that the reference rate proposal could never push a government into defending a rate in a way that would induce a crisis, because it implies no obligation to defend any rate at all. Indeed, it might be regarded as a means of disciplining intervention in a floating-rate system rather than as a distinct intermediate regime—its only claim to inclusion in the latter is that it requires the authorities to analyze where they believe equilibrium rates are, and to announce their conclusions. But this is precisely what, in a carefully argued essay, Pisani-Ferry and Coeure (1999) identified as one of the key needs for improving traditional surveillance.

Soft Margins

In my first extensive development of the case for "target zones"[1] (Williamson 1983, 1985), I suggested that they might have "soft margins"

---

1. This term was originated by Marcus Fleming and incorporated in Guideline 3 of the guidelines for floating exchange rates that he drafted at the IMF in 1974. At that time, it did not imply any positive obligation to keep exchange rates within the agreed-on target zone, a point stressed by Wim Duisenberg in 1976 in urging his European colleagues to use such an approach within the European Community (see Gros and Thygesen 1992, 39–40). But his

or "soft buffers." The idea was that there should not be an absolute government commitment to defend the edges of the zones; rather, in the event of strong speculative pressures, the government should have the right to announce that it would let the rate go outside the band, while warning the market that it planned to direct policy to bring the rate back within the band, if and when that might prove possible. This proposal rather got lost in the discussion of the late 1980s, but it has recently been revived in two analytical contributions by Leonardo Bartolini and Alessandro Prati (1997, 1998).

Bartolini and Prati formalize the notion of a "soft" target zone as one in which the authorities target a moving average of current and past market exchange rates to remain within a defined band, as opposed to targeting the market exchange rate to remain within a defined zone at all times. In their first paper, they specify the requirement as being to keep the arithmetic average of the exchange rate of the past n periods within a defined, unchanging band. In their second paper, they modify this (following a suggestion of Charles Bean during the discussion of the first paper), to specify the objective as being to keep the geometric average, with exponentially decreasing weights, within the defined band.

In both cases, the effect is to allow the exchange rate to move outside the band in the short run, while maintaining the obligation to hold it within the band in the long run. Bartolini and Prati show that such a policy change can be expected to defuse tensions, especially when shocks to "the fundamentals" are short-lived, so that such a softening of the target zone makes the system significantly less vulnerable to speculative pressure. Or, to look at the same issue from another standpoint, it can provide an alternative to a widening of the band as a mechanism for extending the expected life of a target zone. And they argue that such a policy switch was essentially what happened in the ERM after the crisis of August 1993, and observe that it actually did succeed in defusing tension in the case of the ERM, where exchange rates rapidly returned to their former narrow bands after the widening of the margins.

---

need to emphasize this indicates that it was already being used in a different sense: for example, Paul Volcker (1978) urged reaching "a broad consensus about levels of a few key exchange rates that are not acceptable," but claimed that "target or reference rates . . . imply more confidence about identifying a central tendency or a narrower range of fluctuation than is warranted today."

When Fred Bergsten and I developed the target zone proposal in the early 1980s (Bergsten and Williamson 1983), we used it in a sense intermediate between that which Volcker had advocated and that which he evidently understood target zones to be about; in particular, we urged that parities be adjusted regularly, inter alia, to offset inflation differentials, rather than that exchange rates be used to provide a nominal anchor. Paul Krugman subsequently appropriated the term "target zones" to refer to an ERM-type system in which parities were supposed to be fixed, leading me to adopt Jacob Frenkel's term "crawling bands" for what we had been calling target zones.

As already argued, the basic logic for seeking an intermediate exchange rate system that motivates this essay is the fear that freely floating exchange rates are "badly behaved"; that is, prone to losing touch with the fundamentals, or to becoming misaligned. There is at present no formal way of modeling this type of behavior. Temporary deviations of the fundamentals from their normal values, as hypothesized by Bartolini and Prati, seem about as good a way of introducing such behavior into formal models as we have at this time. Their results suggest that soft buffers to a target zone would be a feasible way of making an intermediate regime more robust to speculative shocks.

A recent essay by Charles Goodhart and P.J.R. Delargy (1998) compares the East Asian crisis with a number of crises under the classical gold standard. It argues that one of the factors that helped economies recover under the classical gold standard was the widespread expectation that the exchange rate would revert to its pre-crisis parity once the crisis was over, which avoided widespread insolvencies such as those that resulted from magnification of the burden of foreign debt when the East Asian currencies were devalued. This is a feature that could be replicated by a target zone with soft margins: In a crisis, the currency could be allowed to depreciate, perhaps with some internationally sanctioned right to suspend debt service until normality had been restored, but the expectation would be that the rate would return to its target zone as a part of the process of crisis resolution.

Monitoring Bands

A more recent proposal comes from a committee in India chaired by S.S. Tarapore, a former deputy governor of the Reserve Bank of India (Tarapore Committee 1997). The committee was charged with considering the case for India to move to capital account convertibility.[2] One of their suggestions was that capital account convertibility should be accompanied by the adoption of a "monitoring band" as a framework for exchange rate management.

The center of the monitoring band, which they called the "neutral real effective exchange rate," would again represent an official, and announced, estimate of the equilibrium exchange rate. Within some range around that (they suggested plus or minus 5 percent), there should be a rule that the central bank would not intervene in the market. But once the rate went outside that band, on either side, it would be allowed to intervene; in-

---

2. Incidentally, they recommended in May 1997 that India should try to establish capital account convertibility within 3 years. But they also laid down some preconditions, like fiscal discipline and solvent banks, which many observers judged India would be unlikely to fulfill within 3 years, even in the absence of the East Asian crisis; so their advice was not as reckless as it may sound in the aftermath of that crisis.

deed, there could be some presumption that intervention would normally be appropriate. But, once again, there would be no obligation to intervene, thus again avoiding the commitment to defend a publicly announced margin, which has proved such a problem in provoking speculative attacks.

Comparing Intermediate Regimes

Can one say anything about the relative vulnerability to speculative attack of these three alternative intermediate regimes? The reference rate proposal would seem to be the most invulnerable, inasmuch as it implies the least about any positive obligation to try and avoid misalignments. Target zones and crawling bands with soft margins are at the other extreme, for they still imply an obligation to defend the announced bands, even if these are modified in the way suggested by Bartolini and Prati. Or, in the form that I had originally envisaged soft margins, they would give a government the right to cut its losses and stage a temporary retreat if defense fails, but for that to happen there would have to be a defense and an attack that succeeds. Indeed, some might criticize this proposal on the ground that making it easy for an attack to succeed will encourage attacks that the promise of a more robust defense would be capable of deterring. Monitoring bands are in the middle: They lack an obligation to defend a band, but they imply more of a presumption of action to prevent rates from drifting away from equilibrium than does a reference rate.

That is merely one side of the equation. The other is how much impact the regime can be expected to have in preventing rates from drifting away from the estimated equilibrium rate. Is it possible to advance any reasonably convincing propositions on that topic?

Even the reference rate proposal might help to limit misalignments, to the extent that the reason for the extreme weakness of any mechanism to bring exchange rates back toward equilibrium under floating[3] is ignorance of the equilibrium rate on the part of market operators—ignorance that may be rational, given the private cost of seeking such knowledge. If an informed estimate were provided by the authorities as a public good, it would be equally rational for market operators to make use of that information, assuming that they concluded that it was indeed information and not disinformation.

---

3. The preponderance of the evidence suggests that exchange rates typically take something of the order of 4 years to move halfway back toward equilibrium (usually called "purchasing power parity" in this literature). Over time horizons of up to a year, the behavior of a floating exchange rate is better described by a random walk than by any of the macroeconomic models. See Rogoff (1996).

The additional commitment to official action to limit misalignments in the other two systems would presumably reinforce the incentive to take note of the announced estimate of equilibrium. Just how much attention is paid by market operators must be expected to depend on how much credibility the authorities have built up. Those who defend bands even after these have ceased to be consistent with equilibrium must expect future announcements to be treated with contempt by the markets; and because there has now been a long and unfortunate tradition of such actions, it would be naïve to expect a new band system to command a high degree of credibility with the market immediately.

But if a new system involved serious investment in calculating equilibrium rates, and the authorities resisted the temptation to allow political expediency to override analysis, then market operators who challenged those estimates would experience repeated losses, and credibility would be built up over time. As that happened, speculation would become stabilizing, and help the authorities to defend their rates, as modeled by Krugman (1991).

4

Actions to Influence Exchange Rates

Suppose that a country wishes to adopt one of the intermediate regimes discussed in the previous chapter. For the sake of concreteness, let us suppose that it has decided to adopt a monitoring band. The question to be discussed in this chapter is: What policies, beside announcement of the band—that is, the range of exchange rates that the authorities judge to be consistent with the country's fundamentals in the medium term—could help to keep the rate within the band?

Monetary Policy

The classic instrument for managing an exchange rate is monetary policy. A weak currency can be strengthened by higher interest rates, and a strong currency can be dampened by a lower interest rate.[1] The main claim for currency boards is that they provide an institutional mechanism to ensure that this stabilizing feedback rule is implemented systematically. But, al-

---

1. The relevance of this widely held doctrine to the East Asian economies during the 1997 crisis was questioned by Joseph Stiglitz, then chief economist of the World Bank. He reasoned that what interests a lender is the product of the coupon rate times the probability of being paid, and he argued that an increase in the former might so depress the latter as to leave the lender worse off, thus making higher interest rates a counterproductive policy, even so far as defending the exchange rate is concerned.

This thesis was controversial in the context in which it was advanced, and the empirical evidence is contradictory (Ohno, Shirono, and Sisli 1999 found in its favor; but Park, Wang, and Chung 1999, 14, using data for most of the same economies during a similar period, concluded the opposite). Even if it were true in that context, it seems unlikely to be true in general (though perhaps, like the Laffer curve, it comes into its own in extreme situations).

though the rule is stabilizing from the standpoint of defending an exchange rate target, it can be destabilizing to the domestic economy. Indeed, the ability to use monetary policy to stabilize the domestic economy[2] is traditionally regarded as the main virtue of exchange rate flexibility (see Frankel 1999 for an authoritative recent statement). One of the main purposes of the wide band incorporated into the BBC rules is to permit a relaxation of the monetary consequences of a fixed exchange rate, so as to allow monetary policy at least a limited role in domestic stabilization.

In 1987, Marcus Miller and I developed a "blueprint" for policy coordination that sought to reconcile the pursuit of domestic stabilization with the use of monetary policy to defend target zones (Williamson and Miller 1987). The expectation was that at most times exchange rates would be well within their target zones, and monetary policy could be directed to internal stabilization policy. If necessary, however, if the exchange rate were threatening to breach its target zone, the interest rate would be modified with a view to defending the target zone. That is, a country with a weak currency would raise interest rates to encourage appreciation, whereas a country with an excessively strong currency would lower interest rates and expand the money supply to encourage a depreciation. If these changes in monetary policy threatened to push the domestic economy into recession or inflation, respectively, then the blueprint said that the appropriate counter was a change in fiscal policy: fiscal expansion in the first case, fiscal contraction in the second.

I would no longer advocate such a major reliance on monetary policy to achieve exchange rate targets. This is because the blueprint proposal simply did not resonate, and the reason it did not looks more convincing now than it did in 1987. The objection to it was always that effective domestic stabilization required the use of monetary policy exclusively for that purpose, and would be risked by its possible diversion to manage the exchange rate. In 1987, it was also said that fiscal policy could not be fine-tuned in the way necessary to contribute to domestic stabilization, which seemed to me to rest more on a judgment about the unwillingness of politicians to try than the inability of economists to make useful forecasts. But, if the politicians are indeed unwilling to try, as seems to be the case, that is still conclusive. Furthermore, one hates to imagine how much worse Japan's situation would have been in the 1990s if it had been expected to tighten monetary policy to keep the yen within some reasonable range of its FEER, which would presumably have been set somewhere in the vicinity of a hundred yen to the dollar.

I would not wish to withdraw entirely the ideas embodied in the blueprint. The first question that the authorities of a country with an undesir-

---

2. In the Keynesian heyday, domestic stabilization was described as achieving "internal balance;" today, it is usually described as pursuing an inflation target. From the present standpoint, it does not much matter which description one chooses.

ably strong exchange rate should always ask themselves is whether there may be scope to cut interest rates without undermining domestic economic stability. Similarly, countries with weak currencies should consider whether it may not be appropriate to raise interest rates. The point is that one cannot rely on the answers to those questions always being such as to push the currency in the desired direction; the importance of targets other than the exchange rate precludes unlimited use of monetary policy to manage the exchange rate.

Many economists argue that, unless one is prepared to subjugate domestic considerations to exchange rate management, it is pointless to try to manage the exchange rate at all. A standard Mundellian model with perfect capital mobility and an exchange rate that is always pinned down uniquely by "the fundamentals" creates the "impossible trinity": the impossibility of having simultaneously a fixed (or managed) exchange rate, an independent monetary policy, and free capital mobility.

But this theorem is only as robust as its foundations. The usual ground for attack is to argue that capital mobility is still imperfect. That is undoubtedly true, but it is also clear that capital mobility is high enough to pose a policy problem. The more compelling ground for questioning the theorem is the theory of exchange rate determination embodied in it. If exchange rates in fact have the large arbitrary element that the evidence (as I read it) shows they do, then there may well be scope for an active exchange rate policy. The question is: What other instruments might be available, given that the authorities are not prepared to devote monetary policy primarily to exchange rate management?

Sterilized Intervention

The standard way of seeking to reconcile the use of monetary policy for domestic purposes with the pursuit of an exchange rate target is to resort to sterilized intervention. A country that wishes to prevent its exchange rate from appreciating enters the foreign exchange market to buy dollars in exchange for its domestic currency, but it prevents any net addition to the money supply by simultaneously selling an equivalent volume of treasury bills. In a world without capital mobility, that would enable the central bank to control simultaneously the money supply and the exchange rate.[3] But selling the treasury bills requires an increase in the in-

---

3. Such control might break down in the long run, if the exchange rate were such as to imply a large current account imbalance. In the case of a large deficit, reserves would eventually run out and force abandonment of the exchange rate peg. Even in the surplus case, the ability to sterilize may eventually be called into question, as happened in Germany and Switzerland in the late 1960s.

terest rate, and in a world with a high degree of capital mobility that will attract a further capital inflow.

Indeed, in the limiting case of perfect capital mobility (which is often regarded as an approximation to today's world), sterilization is impossible because the money taken out of circulation through sterilization is simply replaced by a new capital inflow. Even if sterilization is possible, it can be expensive, when the local-currency bonds being issued carry a higher (exchange-rate-adjusted) interest rate than the rate on the reserves that the monetary authority will acquire. For example, Chile estimates that its sterilization efforts cost it about 0.5 percent of GDP in the 1990s (Williamson 1996, 19), and Colombia gives an estimate that in some years sterilization cost as much as 2 percent of GDP (Uribe 1995, 67).

There was a time in the 1980s, epitomized by the Jurgensen Report (1983), when it was fashionable to dismiss the potency of sterilized intervention altogether. Different currencies were argued to be such close substitutes in investors' portfolios that sterilization was impossible. To put it another way, foreign exchange intervention could influence the exchange rate if and only if it were unsterilized, in which case it would also influence the money supply. The only way of controlling the money supply (which was then regarded as an important objective, for that was the heyday of monetarism) was to abandon intervention and allow the exchange rate to float.

Further work since then has cast doubt on this view. Research at the Banca d'Italia (Catte, Galli, and Rebecchini 1994) suggested that intervention, especially when concerted between both the central banks involved, had been quite important in stabilizing the exchange rates between the Group of Three countries' currencies in the period 1985–91 (the post-Plaza period, when free floating among the major countries ceased to be a fetish). The work of Dominguez and Frankel (1993) suggested that, whereas sterilized intervention has a negligible impact through the portfolio channel, it can have an important impact via influencing expectations. If foreign exchange traders revise their forecasts in response to intervention, then it can have a major impact on the exchange rate, whether or not it is sterilized.

Dominguez and Frankel offer several reasons why intervention might sometimes cause traders to revise their exchange rate forecasts. For example, traders might treat intervention as telling them something about likely future monetary policy, or they might expect it to prick what they recognize as a speculative bubble. (An additional reason not noted by Dominguez and Frankel might be if traders knew that the authorities had invested serious effort in analyzing what exchange rate is consistent with the medium-term fundamentals.) The corollary is obviously that the authorities should make their intervention public.

Although work such as that of the Banca d'Italia economists and Dominguez and Frankel has thrown doubt on the proposition that intervention is completely ineffective, economists have not jumped back to the opposite conclusion, that it provides a powerful independent policy weapon for steering exchange rates. In part, doubtless, the limited effectiveness of intervention is attributable to the halfhearted way in which it is typically done. One aspect of this is that the scale of intervention is simply too small to have much impact. The other aspect is that most intervention is done unilaterally by the party that has an obvious immediate interest in limiting the perverse exchange rate change originating in the market.

Cooperative intervention by the authorities on both sides of the market is more effective than unilateral intervention, especially when the latter is undertaken by the weak-currency country (Catte, Galli, and Rebecchini 1994). Indeed, Peter Bofinger (1999) advocates unlimited intervention undertaken by the strong-currency country as the natural weapon to enforce a mutually agreed-on band between the dollar and the euro. Because there is no automatic limit on how much a strong-currency country can intervene, this would provide a degree of credibility that is not achievable when intervention is expected to be undertaken by only one party, especially the weak-currency one.

Although Bofinger was thinking of how one might defend a target zone for the dollar-euro rate, his approach could be of much wider applicability. One might, for example, ask whether the East Asian crisis would not have been ameliorated had the major financial powers chosen to intervene on their own account on a large scale in the second half of 1997 to back a judgment that the exchange rates of the East Asian victims of the crisis had massively overshot. (Their taxpayers would also have benefited, given the subsequent recovery in the exchange rates in question.)

Other Policy Weapons

In view of the facts that sterilization of capital inflows can be expensive and that supportive intervention by the strong-currency country cannot be guaranteed, it is of obvious importance to consider what other policy weapons may be available to a country that is seeking to defend itself against excessive capital inflows.

One possibility is to vary the reserve ratio required of the commercial banks. This can be of particular relevance in helping to combat an unwanted surge of capital inflows. A higher required reserve ratio will have the effect of limiting the monetary expansion that results from any given increase in the monetary base, and, more specifically, will help to prevent bank lending getting out of hand. It will also increase the differential between the interest rate charged to domestic borrowers from the banks and the international interest rate, thus diminishing the incentive for further capital inflows intermediated through the banks.

The problem is that high reserve ratios impose costs of their own: They diminish the efficiency of the financial system as borrowers are diverted away from those lenders subject to the high reserve requirement and toward others that escape that requirement, thus threatening disintermediation. Although it will be worthwhile to accept some disintermediation, these costs place a limit on the extent to which it is prudent to raise reserve requirements.

Another way of achieving de facto sterilization without issuing additional bonds is to require government-controlled financial institutions (such as the postal savings system) to switch their deposits from commercial banks to the central bank. Although this has proved effective in some Asian countries (Fischer and Reisen 1992), it implies either reducing the return to savers in those institutions or (if the central bank pays the normal domestic interest rate) still imposing a cost on the central bank.

A different approach to a large capital inflow is to liberalize current account transactions, for example, by reducing import restrictions. This is a very sensible policy reaction in a country that is still limiting imports more than it regards as in its national interest, for example, because it used to have balance of payments concerns—which is why this was a very important mechanism in postwar Europe during its recovery phase. But once import restrictions have been reduced to the level that appears optimal from a national standpoint, given commercial policy in the rest of the world, it would be costly for the policy to be pushed further. It would not be sensible to vary import restrictions every time the exchange rate deviated from its FEER. Thus this policy is not of much relevance in today's world.

A more relevant option today may be to liberalize capital outflows. Admittedly, there is some reason to worry that a blanket relaxation of capital outflow controls can have the perverse effect of stimulating net inflows (Labán and Larraín 1997; Bartolini and Drazen 1997). The reason is that one of the deterrents to putting money in a country is the fear that it may be difficult to withdraw it again, and so relieving that fear may encourage an inflow. Even so, there will often be scope for limited liberalization of outflows—for example, of foreign direct investment (FDI) or by permitting domestic pension funds to invest abroad—that will be both fairly sure to be helpful in alleviating the pressure of capital inflows, as well as promising welfare benefits in the longer term. The main reason for caution is the fear that these measures will prove irreversible and will provide a source of additional outflows at a time of capital flow reversal.

A very popular recommendation of economists in response to large capital inflows is to tighten fiscal policy. This was indeed recommended by the blueprint referred to above: It would allow interest rates to be reduced without threatening to overheat the domestic economy. It has sometimes been objected that the policy could have the perverse effects of strengthening the confidence of foreign investors and thus adding to the capital inflow, despite a lower domestic interest rate. My own view is that this is farfetched: Capital inflows are unlikely to start on a large scale until the foreign investment community is satisfied that a country's fiscal situation is reasonably sound, and further marginal improvements beyond that are unlikely to outweigh the interest rate impact. The main limitation on this policy comes rather, I would argue, from political economy considerations. It must be difficult for an official to convince a minister of finance, or for a minister of finance to convince his colleagues (or the public), that the rational response to an increased foreign desire to lend to his country is to increase taxes or curtail public expenditures. ("You mean I must raise taxes or cut spending because foreigners are so keen to lend us money?") So I am all for giving the advice to tighten fiscal policy, but realism suggests that we should not expect too much action on this front.

Rather than tighten fiscal policy, a government might seek institutional measures designed to increase private savings. It might, for example, seek to promote a postal savings system, or else establish a system for the private provision of pensions. This helped raise savings in Chile, although mainly because it was decided to finance the transition to the new system (the period when the old state system still has to pay out pensions even though it is no longer receiving contributions) by increasing the regular fiscal surplus rather than by increasing government borrowing. In other words, it was not so much the private pension system per se that increased savings in Chile, as the fact that its introduction provided the occasion for a tightening of fiscal policy.

Finally, there may be scope to discourage capital inflows by withdrawing measures that inadvertently (or, for that matter, deliberately) subsidize inward investment. The two most common examples are probably insurance of bank deposits and grants to direct investors. The case for insuring bank deposits owned by foreigners is weak, and it is easy to recommend that any such insurance should be withdrawn. Grants to direct investors may have a stronger rationale, if they are intended to attract FDI because of its job-creating or technology-enhancing features; but it is healthy to at least ask whether such subsidies are getting value for money. Some, such as tax holidays, are usually just a waste of taxpayers' money; however, by the same count, their withdrawal cannot be expected to do much to diminish the capital inflow.

Capital Controls

Although the preceding battery of instruments may all have a role to play in helping the authorities discourage an exchange rate from moving further outside a monitoring band, none of them is sufficiently powerful to guarantee success (assuming, that is, that the authorities are not prepared to subjugate domestic economic management to defense of the exchange rate). Hence it is natural also to consider whether the use of controls intended to influence capital flows may have a useful role to play.[4]

For a time, in the mid-1990s, all forms of capital control fell into official disfavor. The IMF even debated amending its Articles of Agreement to give it authority over countries' policies with regard to capital controls, with a strong presumption that its objective would be to persuade countries to gradually (or perhaps not so gradually) open their capital accounts (Michel Camdessus, "The IMF Way to Open Capital Accounts," *Wall Street Journal*, 27 September 1995, A14). The basic argument was that capital markets provide an efficient mechanism for determining the allocation of investment, and that any interference with the market mechanism will create distortions that jeopardize economic efficiency. Why should there be any less enthusiasm for the market solution in the capital market than in the goods market, where most economists agree on the virtues of free trade?

Opinion swung back rapidly after the onset of the Asian crisis.[5] The theoretical arguments about capital markets suffering from problems of asymmetric information and moral hazard suddenly seemed far more persuasive than stories about how capital markets were just like any other markets. Jagdish Bhagwati (1998) was particularly vehement in denouncing the proposition that the welfare case for free capital markets was as convincing, in either theoretical or empirical terms, as that for free trade.

In recent years, several authors have sought evidence that would illuminate whether an open capital account increases a country's income. As of now, there have been at least three empirical studies along these lines. Two of them failed to detect any benefit from overall capital account liberalization in terms of the promotion of a faster rate of growth (Alesina, Grilli, and Milesi-Ferretti 1994; Rodrik 1998), whereas one (Quinn 1997) found a positive impact.

It is natural to ask whether it is possible to explain these apparently contradictory findings. In my view, the key lies in recognizing that there is an important difference in the specification of capital account openness between the two studies that found no impact versus that of the Quinn study that did. The first two studies both used a variable that measured whether the capital account was open or closed,[6] whereas Quinn sought

---

4. I do not include the Tobin tax among the potentially useful forms of capital control. This is because I perceive the problem to be an excessive propensity to build up large stocks of short-term assets when times are good, which would not be significantly discouraged by a Tobin tax because they can be rolled over without going through the foreign exchange market, rather than excessive market turnover.

5. But opinion did not swing back as rapidly as one might have expected. The Interim Committee actually gave the go-ahead to proceed with amendment of the Articles during the World Bank-IMF Annual Meetings in Hong Kong in September 1997.

6. Rodrik took the proportion of years in which the capital account was free of restrictions to get a measure that varied between 0 and 1, but the test was whether the capital account was completely free of restrictions.

to construct a measure of the *degree* to which the capital account was open (using data from the IMF's annual report *Exchange Arrangements and Exchange Restrictions*).[7]

Now, most countries have liberalized FDI relatively early on, and most also liberalized long-term before short-term capital. We have strong reasons for believing that liberalization of FDI, portfolio equity, and long-term capital should be beneficial for growth; it is what is usually the last stage—of opening up to unlimited flows of short-term money—that is problematic. Many of Quinn's observations were presumably drawn from episodes where there is a strong probability of benefits being positive, so it is not surprising that he finds a positive effect. In contrast, Alesina, Grilli, and Milesi-Ferretti and Rodrik tested whether complete liberalization is beneficial, and they find no evidence that it is. These findings are thus consistent with the view that opening to FDI and so forth is helpful, whereas exposure to the free flow of short-term financial capital is harmful.

That appeared to be the presumption that underlay Malaysia's imposition of temporary capital controls on 1 September 1998, controls that prohibited the withdrawal of financial capital for 1 year but took care to avoid penalizing FDI. The consequences of this decision have not yet been subject to rigorous academic scrutiny. So far, it is clear that the controls did not have the calamitous effect on business confidence that was so confidently predicted by critics at the time. Malaysia appears to be recovering from the East Asian collapse about as fast as its neighbors (other than Indonesia), rather than having got an extra fillip—as was presumably the intention. But some people argue that the real purpose of the controls was to avoid capital flight developing when Anwar Ibrahim was arrested the day after the controls were imposed, and they were certainly successful in that. The provisional conclusion is that controls on capital outflows can be of help in preventing the start of a panic.

However, most economists have for some years tended to argue that inflow controls are in most cases more likely to be effective than outflow controls, because the incentives for evasion are typically so much greater in the case of outflows. The first point to make concerning the form that any controls should take is that a strong system of prudential supervision of the financial system—one that places strict limits on the ability of financial institutions to hold unmatched currency positions—may well be the most effective single deterrent to excessive foreign borrowing. Moreover, a well-regulated, well-supervised financial system can also limit the damage that is done if a currency crisis does nevertheless occur. Prudential supervision is, one might say, a no-brainer.

---

7. A second difference concerns the sample of countries: 20 OECD countries in the case of Alesina, Grilli, and Milesi-Ferretti; a mixed panel of 64 developing and industrial countries in the case of Quinn; and a large panel of exclusively developing countries in the case of Rodrik.

But it is not necessarily enough. The corporate sector can borrow abroad on its own account, as was the major factor in Indonesia. Or the corporate sector may be willing to take foreign-exchange-denominated loans from the banks, which leaves the banks with a position that is at least nominally covered. One should recognize also that a well-supervised financial system is likely to increase the attraction of a country as a destination for loose capital.

For these reasons, there may still be a role for capital inflow controls. When one asks what sort of inflow controls seem to have worked well in the 1990s, by discouraging inflows of short-term capital but not that in other forms, many economists have argued that the obvious example to emulate is Chile. Between 1991 and 1999, Chile has imposed an unremunerated reserve requirement (URR)[8] designed to discourage the sort of short-term money whose panic withdrawal was mainly responsible for creating such havoc in East Asia, as well as a minimum holding period of 1 year for equity investments.

Paradoxically, despite the widespread commendation of the Chilean model, most of the recent academic literature examining the efficacy of Chile's URR varies from skeptical to negative. For example, Salvador Valdes-Prieto and Marcelo Soto (1998, 152) cite their own finding (in a paper in Spanish) that the URR "did not influence the path of the real exchange rate even in the short run," and in their summary (1998, 133) state that the URR "did not discourage total net short-term credit inflows to the private sector" and "failed to contribute to monetary autonomy." Sebastian Edwards (1999, 24) says that his results "provide preliminary evidence suggesting that the impact of [the URR] on the real exchange rate has been very limited and short-lived," which "confirms" the Valdes-Prieto and Soto findings, and that "the restrictions on capital inflows . . . had a small and temporary effect on interest rate behavior in Chile."

Francisco Nadal-De Simone and Piritta Sorsa (1999, 1) conclude that it "seems premature to view the Chilean experience as supportive of controls on capital inflows." Bernard Laurens and Jaime Cardoso (1998, 4) tell us that the results from their empirical tests suggest that the URR "had no long-term effect on total [capital] inflows, the exchange rate, or domestic interest rates." The one dimension on which just about all investigators agree that the URR has been effective is in extending the maturity of Chile's foreign debt, although some investigators argue that even on this count the effect has been rather modest.

Perhaps the most extreme assertions about the ineffectiveness of capital controls have been made by Laurens and Cardoso (1998). If they are right in claiming that these controls have had no impact on anything much ex-

---

8. Known in Spanish as the *encaje*.

cept the labeling of capital inflows,[9] then one could argue that the URR shares the great virtue of Henry George's tax on land values, in raising revenue without distorting behavior. It does raise a significant amount of revenue: 0.1 to 0.2 percent of GDP, according to Guillermo Le Fort and Sergio Lehmann (2000, 3). Although this is less than the cost of sterilizing capital inflows, which is estimated by the central bank as 0.5 percent of GDP, it is a worthwhile sum. Even if the URR affected neither total capital inflows, nor the exchange rate, nor domestic interest rates, it would have to be judged a great success.

But of course one needs to ask whether it is really true that the URR was as ineffective as claimed. Let us first examine the basis for Edwards' claim that the URR had no significant, long-lived impact on the real exchange rate. This assertion is based on a comparison of VARs (vector autoregressions) explaining exchange rate determination for two different periods, one with and the other without capital controls. Edwards (1999, 24) tells us that if the policy were effective "one would expect that the real exchange rate response to a capital flow innovation would be less pronounced . . . in the period with controls," which it was not. However, his question is wrongly posed: The question is not whether the response to a capital flow innovation differs under these two regimes, but whether *the innovations in capital flows* would differ. If the URR has an impact on capital flows, then it can still influence the exchange rate, even if the relationship between a given capital flow and the exchange rate remains unchanged (which is what I would in fact expect to be the case).

Another of his claims is that the URR had only a small and temporary effect on interest rates. He starts by stating that the equilibrium interest differential

$$r - r^* - E(de) = k + R + u \tag{1}$$

where r is the domestic interest rate, r^* is the world interest rate, $E(de)$ is the expected rate of devaluation, k is the tax equivalence of the capital restrictions, R is the country risk premium, u is an i.i.d. (independently and identically distributed) random variable, and time subscripts have been suppressed. It would seem difficult to quarrel with this equation, which says that the URR introduced a permanent differential between domestic

---

9. There is general agreement that the URR prompted attempts at evasion. Nadal-De Simone and Sorsa (1999) trace how the URR stimulated substantial shifting of capital flows: away from the targeted short-term flows, first to secondary American depositary receipts, then to FDI, and then to trade credits (for which domestic financing has been declining, despite a continued robust growth of trade) and perhaps trade misinvoicing (which, they claim, could be disguising capital inflows of as much as 2 percent of GDP per year). This response of the capital markets in turn stimulated the authorities into a series of extensions of the scope of the URR.

and world interest rates unless either k diminished to zero or it was offset one-for-one by a decline in the country risk premium.

Edwards does not claim that k disappeared over time because the market became so clever at evading the controls. On the contrary, his table 7 demonstrates that this did not happen, because it shows the value of the unremunerated reserves rising almost monotonically from 1991 to 1996. Had the URR caused an equivalent decline in the country risk premium R, it would surely have deserved even more praise as an efficient way of raising taxation than was argued above, for this would imply that it transferred income from foreigners to Chile, without diminishing foreign welfare and without causing any economic distortions.

But Edwards does not make any such implausible claim. Instead, he again estimates a pair of VAR equations that contrast the dynamic adjustment of interest rates without and with capital controls. Because the two are rather similar, with the speed of adjustment being only slightly slower with the URR, he claims that this shows that the URR "had a small and temporary effect on interest rate behavior in Chile" (Edwards 1999, 33). But this is wrong; what it shows is that interest rate convergence to equilibrium was similar, but not that interest rates converged to the same level, which equation (1) tells us they did not, and which is the important issue.

Jose De Gregorio, Sebastian Edwards, and Rodrigo Valdes (2000) also conclude that the URR had only temporary effects on interest rates, plus an important impact on the composition of foreign borrowing. However, the reason they conclude that the impact of the URR on interest rates was only temporary is that the shocks to the URR are temporary (in part because evasion builds up over time, until the authorities amend the rules to plug new loopholes that the private sector has discovered). Under the assumption of a permanent shock, a 30 percent URR is estimated to increase the domestic interest rate between 130 and 150 basis points (De Gregorio, Edwards, and Valdes 2000, 17). So far as reserve composition is concerned, they examine international data (to avoid the suspicion that the impact on composition shown by national data is biased by the relabeling of flows) and show that Chile is seventh, out of 31 countries, in terms of both a small fraction of short-term debt and a reduction in the share of short-term debt since 1990.

Edwards (1999) also agrees that the URR had an impact on the composition of capital inflows, tilting them toward longer-term flows (notably FDI). The findings that the URR had an impact on interest rates and the composition of capital inflows, but not on the total level of capital inflows or on the exchange rate, is in fact typical of this literature. Francisco Gallego, Leonardo Hernandez, and Klaus Schmidt-Hebel (1999, 3) summarize thus: "In sum, there is robust evidence showing that the URR has led to higher domestic interest rates . . . and a composition of inflows biased toward longer maturities. However, the effect of the URR on the real exchange rate . . . has proved to be more difficult to uncover, most likely due to difficulties in finding the correct model that relates these two . . . variables."[10] A more recent paper dissents from what had begun to look like a (theoretically implausible) consensus of the empirical work, that the URR did not reduce the total capital inflow, and finds a robust impact (Le Fort and Lehmann 2000).

Since it is a well-known fact that empirical exchange rate models do not work (Meese and Rogoff 1983), a failure to find a role for the URR in such models is indeed hardly decisive. But there is another possible explanation of the findings. Let us grant that the URR did indeed give the Central Bank of Chile the latitude to raise interest rates (corrected for expected exchange rate changes and the country risk premium) above the world level. If it chose to use its freedom to raise interest rates, then we would expect investigators to observe the higher interest differential that they report having found.

But in that case there is little reason to expect the total size of the capital inflow to be reduced by the URR, and it is only if the capital flow equation included an interest differential term (as in Le Fort and Lehmann 2000) that it would detect an impact of the URR on the capital inflow. And if the capital inflow is the same, then any impact on the exchange rate would be restricted to that which stems from the impact of the higher interest rates on domestic demand and via that on the current account deficit, which one would expect to be a second-order effect. In other words, the empirical findings seem consistent with the view that the URR was effective, plus the hypothesis that the Chilean authorities chose to use the leeway it provided to raise interest rates rather than to limit the size of the capital inflow.

Some of the other criticisms of the Chilean controls made in this literature seem quite wrongheaded. In particular, Laurens and Cardoso (1998) ask whether the controls bought time, and answer that they did not, on the ground that Chile made no progress in reducing the interest differential vis-à-vis the rest of the world during the period 1992–97. Another way of expressing the same finding of fact would be that the URR enabled Chile to maintain an interest differential continuously during that period, rather than that it was eroded down (as would have been true had all the effects been short-lived). They criticize Chile for having reduced the URR to zero, rather than abolishing it, when hit by the fallout from the Asian crisis. This shows that Chile regards the URR as a "device to counteract the effects of shifts in market sentiment on the country risk premium in a situation where structural rigidities prevent domestic interest rates from adjusting to a new external environment" (Laurens and Cardoso 1998,

10. The empirical findings of Gallego, Hernandez, and Schmidt-Hebel are similar to those they summarize from the preceding literature: The URR raises interest rates (although they seem uncertain whether by 9 basis points, e.g., p. 22, or by 300 basis points, e.g., note 23) and influences the composition of capital inflows, but not total capital inflows or the exchange rate.

20). How naughty of Chile to seek to insulate its economy from foreign shocks, instead of making sure its economy bobs around naturally in the choppy seas of international finance!

My conclusion is that much of the literature on the Chilean URR has exaggerated its ineffectiveness. Apart from its impact in extending the maturity of the debt, which is generally acknowledged, the bulk of the evidence (as summarized in Nadal-De Simone and Sorsa 1999 and Ariyoshi et al. 2000) suggests that there is an impact on the interest rate. The puzzle in the literature is that so many authors (and the summaries just cited) go on to claim at most that "there is mixed and weak evidence that the URR has reduced the magnitude of capital inflows and actually no evidence that the URR has affected the level of the real exchange rate" (Ariyoshi et al. 2000, 10). These findings are simply inconsistent. There is no remotely plausible model under which the URR could influence interest rates but not be capable of influencing capital flows; that would require that capital flows not be influenced by the interest differential. Similarly, there is no remotely plausible model under which capital flows have no impact on the exchange rate.

What these empirical findings may reflect is that the impact of the URR was small relative to the noise in the determination of capital flows and (what is entirely unsurprising, given the state of the art) the exchange rate. One may surmise that one reason for this is that a foreign investor acquires a right to keep his money in short-term assets in Chile after he has once paid the URR (Herrera and Valdes 1999). This option right means that the true impact of the URR on k in equation (1) above is substantially exaggerated by the sort of simple static calculation that most analysts have employed. This might suggest that the URR was set at too low a rate to achieve all that was asked of it: Indeed, defenders of the URR have argued that the Chilean authorities erred in failing to raise it to counter the capital surge of 1996–97 (Agosin and Ffrench-Davis 1999; Le Fort and Lehmann 2000).

Richard Cooper (1999) pointed out that large premiums have often developed in the presence of capital controls, a fact that is inconsistent with the contention that such controls are totally ineffective. That is not to claim that capital controls are leak-proof, just that the leaks are sufficiently small to make the vessel still capable of carrying a worthwhile volume of water.

I do not find that recent Chilean literature overturns my prior belief that capital controls can be a useful complement to macroeconomic policies designed to limit counterproductive movements in the exchange rate. Their main danger is that they may tempt governments into excessive reliance on them: Capital controls can only sensibly be used as an adjunct to, rather than a substitute for, "sound policies" (which is trite, though one would not think so, given the vehemence with which the point is made in much of the literature).

There is widespread agreement among economists that capital controls that alter the terms on which transactions can be undertaken (so-called price-related measures) are preferable to prohibitions and quantitative controls. This is because price-related measures allow agents to determine for themselves whether or not a particular transaction is worth undertaking, and such decentralization of decision making permits an aggregate target to be achieved at the lowest social cost.

The URR is the most familiar measure that falls into this category, but it should not be taken for granted that it is the only, or the best, such measure. In particular, a recent paper by Howell Zee (1999) argues the merits of a cross-border capital tax, which is intended to fulfill the same role as the URR. The tax would be levied by financial institutions on a withholding basis on all receipts of foreign exchange. It could then be refunded on exports through the value-added tax system, and on receipts of income through the income tax system. He argues that this system would be administratively simpler and far more resistant to evasion than the Chilean URR. It is an argument that deserves to be given careful consideration by countries that are threatened with excessive capital inflows and are contemplating the use of capital inflow taxes in response.

5

Managed Floating

Many economies, including most of the East Asian ones except Hong Kong and Malaysia, now describe their exchange regimes as involving "independent floating"; but they do not appear to interpret this as precluding them from intervening heavily with a view to trying to influence what happens to their exchange rate. Certainly South Korean intervention is reported to have been very heavy during the winter of 1999–2000, and, from press accounts, was clearly directed at limiting the appreciation of the won, as well as at rebuilding reserves.

This is what is meant by "managed floating": where the authorities of a country do not announce any objectives that would permit a judgment that they had succeeded or failed, but where they nevertheless have views about where the exchange rate ought (or ought not) to be, and are prepared to act on those views. They announce no parity or band, but they typically worry if the rate depreciates a lot, and they intervene, or change interest rates, or sometimes seek to influence the flow of capital, with a view to having an impact on the exchange rate. And they may certainly worry about the exchange rate appreciating so much as to threaten their economy's trade competitiveness, as has been the case in South Korea.

Managed floating is another intermediate exchange rate regime. It is therefore of interest to ask how it compares with the more formal regimes already discussed, namely the reference rate proposal, soft bands, and monitoring bands. Unfortunately, this is not an easy question to answer, because managed floating is not a regime with well-defined rules, and there is no statistical database on how managed floats have behaved that can be exploited to perform empirical tests. But obviously any comparison with the formal intermediate regimes will depend on the strategy that a country managing its float chooses to adopt. The first issue is therefore to try and characterize the possible alternative strategies. At least five come to mind.

Alternative Strategies

One possible strategy has tended to be popular with academics: The authorities would "lean against the wind" by buying reserves when the domestic currency was appreciating and selling when it was depreciating, without making any attempt to form a judgment as to whether the rate was overvalued or undervalued. A second, which seems to have been quite popular with central banks, may be termed the "fixed but adjustable-under-market-pressure peg": The authorities hold the rate roughly constant until market pressures build up, when they allow it to move until the pressures subside, at which point they again stabilize it in a new range until some new market pressures emerge. A third strategy would be to seek to defend an unannounced crawling band (this is the "quiet band" advocated by Goldstein 1995).

A fourth strategy would be to operate an unannounced reference rate, tending to intervene with a view to depreciating the currency when it is stronger than some unannounced target and with a view to appreciating the currency when it is weaker than this target.[1] A fifth strategy would be to start such intervention only when the exchange rate had deviated by more than some threshold away from the unannounced reference rate, which would amount to operating an unannounced monitoring band. Doubtless, management may at times be less systematic than is implied by any of these descriptions, but that makes it impossible to develop any systematic comparison with the more formal intermediate regimes.[2]

The first strategy is fundamentally different from the other four, in that it envisages systematic intervention without the need for the authorities to make a decision on what exchange rate they deem to be appropriate, in the sense of consistent with the fundamentals. This was the first interpretation that was given to the concept of managed floating, by Paul Wonnacott (1965). It is a policy that has never appealed to me. If one believes that

---

1. This has sometimes been described as "leaning against the wind," but it is conceptually quite distinct from the first strategy listed above. In particular, this does, and the first does not, require the authorities to have in mind some notion of the equilibrium rate.

2. The lack of any statistical database on currencies with managed floating precludes any test of the adequacy of ad hoc management in curbing misalignments. My impression is that central banks that are managing their currencies without any publicly-announced obligations tend to limit short-run volatility quite effectively, but most of them seem to be periodically obliged to allow fairly large changes in response to market forces, which suggests that they usually operate something like the adjustable-under-market-pressure type of system.

the market is forward-looking and rational, then one would not want to intervene at all: Free floating is the preferred policy. But if one is fearful that the market sometimes takes rates to misaligned levels, then one surely wants to try and correct any misalignment as rapidly as possible: To intervene to slow a movement back toward equilibrium from an overvalued or undervalued level is perverse. Only if one believes that rapid change, rather than misalignment, is a policy problem, is it conceivable that a strategy of "leaning against the wind" might make sense.

The other four of the five systematic strategies described above are simply analogues of familiar intermediate regimes, in which the policy is unannounced to the market. They amount to, respectively, an unannounced adjustable peg, an unannounced crawling band, an unannounced reference rate, and an unannounced monitoring band. Hence, these four regimes can be evaluated essentially by asking whether it is better for the authorities to try and inform the market of what they are doing or not.

Announcement

In the case of the adjustable peg, it is easy to believe in the virtue of not announcing policy. Because any correctly anticipated parity change guarantees a speculative profit for the market at the expense of the authorities (i.e., the taxpayers), it is better not to give the market correct information about future policy. Of course, the fact that this makes the system inherently crisis-prone is one of the chief charges against it.

A crawling band, even with soft margins, would also have some potential for provoking crises. In my original version, where the authorities would have the right to suspend defense of the margins in the event of strong speculative pressures, there would have to be a mini-crisis to provide the occasion for suspending the margins. In Bartolini and Prati's (1998) version, pressures would arise if the rate went and stayed significantly outside the medium-term band for a prolonged period, and the market then realized that the authorities would have to engineer a strong recovery to respect their obligation to hold the medium-term average within the specified band. In neither case would the system be crisis-proof, which would make some sort of a case for preserving confidentiality. This would need to be weighed against the benefit of focusing expectations when the band is not suspect.

But no similar case can be constructed for keeping the market in ignorance of the other two regimes. Neither a reference rate nor a monitoring band imposes any obligation to defend a particular rate; hence, it is impossible for either of them to precipitate a crisis. The only question that arises in these cases is to what extent the provision of information to the market concerning the authorities' estimates of equilibrium, and therefore the direction in which the authorities' actions will tend to push the rate, can be expected to help focus stabilizing expectations. Because there is no experience with either a reference rate or a monitoring band, there is no evidence to which one can appeal to establish how important such an effect might be. Nevertheless, it is obviously better to pick a system with an upside and no downside than one with neither upside nor downside. That says that one should announce policy.

Where there is genuine ambiguity is in choosing between a relatively hard but quiet band, on the one hand, versus a reference rate or monitoring band, on the other. If one believes that the authorities can usually do a pretty good job of managing the rate except when strong market pressures develop, it may make sense to give them the latitude to manage as they see fit—coupled with the escape valve of being able to withdraw when they consider that advisable. If one can rely on the authorities assuring themselves that any new rate at which they might choose to stabilize is consistent with the fundamentals, one might even use this to rationalize a peg that is temporarily fixed but adjustable under strong market pressure, in preference to a reference rate or monitoring band.

However, the proviso about the need to be able to rely on the good judgment of the authorities is key, because one characteristic of managed floating is a lack of transparency. One cannot rely on informed public discussion of policy to illuminate its failings or suggest improvements, because the public is not provided with information on which it can judge whether the authorities' aims are sensible, or whether they are succeeding in implementing those aims. This lack of transparency is the second major inadequacy of managed floating, alongside its failure to provide the market with any focus for stabilizing speculation.

Or is the lack of transparency a disadvantage? Naturally think-tankers think it is, but government officials tend to take a very different view. They find it attractive to be able to act without the threat of informed criticism. They surely find life easier when there are no public benchmarks that can indicate their failure. They run much less risk of political censure when misalignments can be blamed on the anonymous market than when the headlines are prone to scream that their policies have failed. So it is not very difficult to understand the charm of managed floating to an insider.

What seems much stranger is that many academics are so tolerant of the lack of transparency of managed floating in an age when transparency has emerged as a litmus test of public institutions. A possible explanation is that not all have yet caught up with the reality reflected in Calvo and Reinhart's (2000) analysis of "fear of floating"—namely, that most countries that describe their policies as floating do not in fact resign themselves to allowing the market to work its will unimpeded.

One might conjecture that these academics support free floating because they assume that the exchange markets work like the textbooks say they do, with ubiquitous rational expectations pinning down exchange rates to levels determined by "the fundamentals." This is often regarded as desirable not just because "the market knows best," but also because (like a currency board) free floating eliminates any role for discretionary policy. Managed floating then is accepted as a mildly degraded version of the real thing, which shares the virtue of being relatively immune to speculative crises—which is, after all, the major factor that has driven many to advocate the "two corners" position.

Let us instead be realistic enough to accept the fact that few countries feel comfortable abandoning their exchange rate to either the workings of the free market or permanent fixity. Most governments and central banks believe that they can bring to bear something that the markets lack, namely, a focus on longer-term issues. My own view is that this is entirely reasonable. But then one needs to ask whether exchange rate policy should be subject to public scrutiny. If one regards that as desirable, managed floating is ruled out. In addition to providing transparency, a reference rate or monitoring band has the potential to strengthen the incentive for stabilizing speculation, and thus ease the problem posed by excessive capital mobility.

Hence, my recommendation to the emerging markets is to move to one of the formal intermediate regimes. The key step would be to make a public announcement of their reference rate, or parity (center of the band). My preference between the options would be for a monitoring band, on the ground that this gives rather more guidance to the market as to when it can expect official action to limit misalignments to kick in while eliminating the risk of a speculative attack. But this is not a strongly held preference. Managed floating may not be a greatly inferior option if the management is done according to the same principles, although it suffers from the twin disadvantages of nontransparency and of wasting the opportunity to harness market forces in support of stabilizing speculation. Unfortunately, many officials view that lack of transparency as the charm of floating.

6

Concluding Remarks

The argument of this essay may be summarized as follows. Apart from the handful of countries that feel comfortable with a hard peg, the emerging markets have been forced by a combination of events and pressure from the Group of Seven countries (G-7) and the IMF to float. This is primarily because of a belief that "a flexible exchange rate regime allows large adverse shocks to be more easily deflected or absorbed than a pegged or quasi-pegged exchange rate regime" (Mussa et al. 2000, 38). Floating also gives agents an incentive to cover their foreign exchange exposure, thus making it less likely that a big depreciation will result in a major crisis.

Nevertheless, most of the emerging-market countries (the East Asians perhaps more than the Latin Americans) are reluctant floaters, at least if one assumes that "proper" floating is that practiced by the G-7. They do not exhibit what is always referred to in the literature as "benign neglect" toward the exchange rate, although what is supposed to be benign about it is not obvious, given the evidence as to how unmanaged exchange rates behave. I have argued that their behavior is motivated not by an irrational fear of floating, but by legitimate concerns that floating will generate misalignments that would prevent a resumption of the stellar economic performance of East Asia during the quarter-century before the 1997 crisis.

What happens in practice in this situation is that countries resort to managed floating. This has two disadvantages: that its lack of transparency raises the risk of opportunistic behavior at cross-purposes between different countries, and that it forgoes the chance to provide a focus for expectations that might make private speculation more stabilizing. The question is whether it might be possible to find an alternative regime that would perform better on one or both of those dimensions. I have argued that it would in fact be possible to design a viable intermediate regime that would further both objectives.

In particular, a publicly announced monitoring band[1] could still provide market guidance for where exchange rates are likely to be in the longer term, and one could hope that this might provide a focus for stabilizing market expectations. A monitoring band would provide information to the market as to what rate the authorities believe to be consistent with the long-term fundamentals, and hence as to where to expect official action intended to limit misalignment. But, because it would not impose an obligation on the authorities to defend a Maginot line, it should be immune from the crises that have plagued intermediate regimes, even from the crises of contagion to which it seems that well-managed BBC regimes are subject.

Perhaps it needs to be emphasized that the analysis I have offered differs quite sharply from the traditional analysis of fixed versus flexible exchange rates. Take the treatment of Frankel as an authoritative recent presentation of the traditional approach. He states (1999, 8):

> The two big advantages of a fixed exchange rate . . . are: (1) that it reduces transactions costs and exchange-rate risk which can discourage trade and investment, and (2) that it provides a credible nominal anchor for monetary policy. The big advantage of a floating exchange rate is that it enables a country to pursue an independent monetary policy.

Frankel contends that most evidence has tended to downplay the importance of exchange rate risk in curbing international integration, although he also points to one study which suggests that the benefits of going all the way to monetary union may be greater than has usually been concluded. He asserts that most economists who favor fixed rates do so instead because they attach primary importance to the argument that this provides a clear, easily monitored commitment to anchor monetary policy, and thus pin down the indeterminacy in the absolute price level that is present in any respectable monetary model with its property of zero-degree homogeneity of all absolute prices.

In contrast, most economists who favor floating rates do so because a floating exchange rate allows monetary policy to be used to steer the domestic economy (Friedman 1953).[2] Given the theorem of the impossible

---

1. Alternative possibilities would be a reference rate or a crawling band with soft margins, perhaps taking the form of a requirement to keep the medium-term average of the market exchange rate within a band.

2. Friedman also attached considerable importance to what he called "the daylight saving argument" for flexible exchange rates. This argued that it was much easier to change one price, namely the exchange rate, than to alter thousands or millions of individual prices, when an economy needed to enhance (or reduce) its international price competitiveness in the interest of balance of payments adjustment.

trinity—the inability to have simultaneously a fixed exchange rate, a national monetary policy, and free capital mobility—it is asserted that the best choice is to give up the fixed exchange rate. (Intermediate regimes are, of course, based on the supposition that it is best to give up a bit of all three; that is, to seek an interior solution.)

The odd thing about these traditional criteria is that they have remarkably little bearing on the concerns that seem to drive most policymakers in choosing between one exchange rate regime and another. If we join Frankel in discounting transactions costs, the only reason left for not floating is the desire to have a nominal anchor, yet recent evidence (from Brazil[3] as well as East Asia) indicates overwhelmingly that the price level is not closely anchored by the exchange rate. One wonders why any policymaker would have a "fear of floating," and yet the evidence is that they do. Nor is there any mention of the relative vulnerability of different regimes to crises, which is surely, in practice, the main factor that has driven countries to adopt floating rates. Thus the traditional criteria offer no insights capable of explaining why the debate on the exchange rate regime has led many analysts to argue that the options have been hollowed out to a choice between the extremes of truly fixed or freely floating rates.

I have argued that the major drawback of freely floating exchange rates concerns neither transactions costs, nor exchange rate risk, nor the lack of a nominal anchor. The problem is rather that the capricious variation in freely floating rates results not just in short-run volatility, which may be a nuisance but can be effectively hedged through forward markets, but also

---

3. Let me use the case of Brazil to illustrate the reasons for my skepticism about the nominal anchor argument. When Brazil stopped inflation in its tracks with the Plano Real in the middle of 1994, the exchange rate was initially allowed to float up rather than be used as a nominal anchor.

After several weeks, the authorities became concerned that the appreciation was becoming excessive, and so they intervened to cap the rise of the real. In due course, they started to allow a very gradual depreciation, so as to limit the loss of competitiveness that was resulting from the much-reduced but still significant inflation, and it gradually became an article of faith that it was the exchange rate that was serving as a nominal anchor. The danger of inducing a renewed acceleration of inflation was given as the reason for rejecting the advice to accelerate the downward crawl, so as to head off the looming prospect of an exploding current account deficit, with the risk, which was realized in January 1999, of a foreign exchange crisis. (The authorities actually decelerated the crawl in the belief that this would speed up the convergence of inflation to the world level.)

But what happened after the crisis and the forced floating of the real, which promptly floated down almost as dramatically as the East Asian currencies did in late 1997? Yes, inflation did accelerate a bit, to about 9 percent in 1999, which is nowhere near enough to eliminate the gain in Brazilian competitiveness, even after the real had recovered from its low point of about R$2.30 to the vicinity of R$1.70 to the dollar. That is a story that is very similar to the experiences of the East Asian economies in 1997–98, where large depreciations also induced only small increases in inflation and left the economies concerned far more competitive than before. It is simply not true that the price level is closely anchored by the exchange rate, as would be necessary to justify the policy advice to use the exchange rate as a nominal anchor.

in long-run misalignments, which can be highly disruptive of good economic performance. Governments and central banks are doubtless very imperfect human institutions, but they can bring a longer-term perspective to the issue of exchange rate determination, and this is needed if misalignments are to be limited to a reasonable range.

The traditional intermediate regime of the BBC rules tried to spell out how the authorities should introduce that long-term perspective in a way that would safeguard the system against speculative attacks, but it turns out that this solution has two weaknesses. First, even a well-managed system is subject to the danger of being sideswiped by contagion. Second, the BBC rules demand a high standard of competence on the part of governments, which is not always present, and its absence feeds the thirst for such automatic systems as currency boards and free floats. That leads to a public relations problem as well: The ideologues of floating willfully lump together the adjustable peg and the BBC rules, and use the predictable failure of the former to dismiss the latter.

It seems clear that emerging-market countries are going to have to learn to live with more flexible exchange rate regimes than most of them have had in the past. But this does not mean that they should be expected to treat their exchange rates with what is often described as benign neglect—though it would be better described as malign neglect: Exchange rates are too important to be left to foreign exchange traders. One can only lament the fact that at present the IMF is misusing its authority to push countries into one of the two corners. It should instead encourage them to adopt monitoring bands or some similar intermediate technique able to ensure that flexible exchange rates are managed transparently so as to focus expectations on a range of rates that make sense in terms of the medium-term fundamentals.

APPENDICES

Appendix 1
Free versus Fearful Floaters

An important new paper by Guillermo Calvo and Carmen Reinhart (2000) analyzes the behavior of exchange rates, reserves, the monetary base, and interest rates in a number of countries that describe their exchange rate regime as one of floating. They take the United States[1] and Japan as providing a calibration of what may be expected in terms of the volatility of these variables under floating rates. The first two rows of table A1.1 show certain of their measures of volatility for the United States and Japan, respectively.[2] The next eight rows show the equivalent figures for eight emerging-market countries that figure in my preceding study, and that describe their regime as one of floating. Three of these describe their float as being managed, while five of them describe themselves as independently floating. The last row shows the equivalent figures for Thailand, a country that described itself as fixing its exchange rate. (It was fixed to a dollar-dominated basket for the later part of this period.)

It can be seen that most of the emerging-market countries with rates described as floating had more volatility than fixed-rate Thailand but less volatility than the United States and Japan. India and South Korea are closer to Thailand than to the benchmark floaters, whereas Malaysia,

---

1. The US exchange rate is taken as the dollar-deutsche mark rate.

2. They calculate other measures as well, e.g., for the probability of monthly changes in the first three variables falling within a range of plus or minus 2.5 percent rather than plus or minus 1 percent, but the general picture is not greatly changed by examining any of these other measures.

Table A1.1   Measures of volatility in countries with floating exchange rates

| Country | Regime description | Probability of monthly changes within plus or minus 1 percent | | | Probability of monthly change in interest rate being less than 25 basis points |
		Exchange rate	Foreign exchange reserves	Monetary base	
United States, 1973–99	Float	26.8[a]	28.6	42.1	59.7
Japan, 1973–99	Float	33.8	44.8	22.7	67.9
India, 1993–99	Float	82.2	21.6	27.4	6.4
South Korea, 1980–97	Managed float	80.1	16.1	12.3	31.1
Malaysia, 1992–98	Managed float	59.4	34.3	24.3	66.7
Mexico, 1994–99	Float	34.6	13.2	5.7	8.3
Peru, 1990–99	Float	45.2	23.1	22.9	24.8
South Africa, 1983–99	Float	32.8	8.7	45.4	35.6
Turkey, 1980–99	Managed float	12.6	10.3	12.2	3.4
Uganda, 1992–99	Float	52.9	17.7	15.6	11.6
Thailand, 1970–97	Fix	93.6	21.3	19.8	24.1

a. Deutsche mark to dollar rate.

Source: Calvo and Reinhart (2000).

Peru, and Uganda are intermediate. Mexico and South Africa have volatility similar to that of Japan. Turkey, which describes its regime as a "managed float," actually had even more volatility than the United States. These results show no obvious relationship between volatility and whether or not a country claims to manage its float.

Observed volatility will depend not merely on a country's policies, as supposedly described by its exchange rate regime, but also on the shocks to which it is subject. Calvo and Reinhart therefore measure also the volatility of foreign exchange reserves, to measure the extent to which a country intervenes in the market to limit movements in its exchange rate. One would expect the United States to have abnormally high volatility on this measure, inasmuch as its reserves are very modest relative to any other relevant magnitude. Nonetheless, US reserves are actually less volatile than those of any other country in the table except Japan and Malaysia. Five of the eight floaters, including three of the five independent floaters, actually show more reserve volatility than fixed-rate Thailand.

Countries may also seek to manage their exchange rate by directing monetary policy to that end. This would result in a high degree of volatility in their monetary base and/or their interest rate, that is, in low numbers in the last two columns of table A1.1. All the emerging-market countries except South Africa show more volatility in their monetary base than the United States, although India, Malaysia, and Peru also show less than Japan (with Thailand quite close as well). In terms of interest rate volatility, however, only Malaysia is at all comparable to the benchmark floaters.

Overall, these results suggest that few of the emerging-market countries that describe themselves as having floating exchange rates are content to allow their rates to float as freely as the United States or Japan do. Malaysia appears to have done the least in terms of intervening or adjusting monetary policy to stabilize its exchange rate, but the fact that the volatility of its exchange rate is so much less than in the US or Japanese cases suggests that it may simply be subject to fewer shocks. Turkey is at the other extreme: Its exchange rate has been very volatile, but so have its other policies, suggesting that it has suffered either strong shocks or frenetic policymakers. The other emerging-market countries all show evidence of having used either intervention or monetary policy or both to limit exchange rate volatility.[3] In the phrase of Calvo and Reinhart, they exhibit "fear of floating" (2000, 2).

---

3. The Mexicans argue that their monetary policy is guided not by a concern to manage the exchange rate, but by their inflation target. A depreciation of the peso threatens to increase inflation, which causes them to raise interest rates (Ortiz and Carstens 2000). It is not clear that this can explain the reserve volatility as well as the volatility in base money and interest rates.

Appendix 2
The Case for a Common Basket Peg
for East Asian Currencies

This appendix reproduces the bulk of a paper that I wrote in 1996 that argued the case for a simultaneous change in the exchange rate peg used by a group of East Asian currencies.[1] I assume for the time being that nine economies would be involved: China, Hong Kong, Indonesia, Malaysia, the Philippines, Singapore, South Korea, Taiwan, and Thailand. The reason for picking this group is the impression that they are close competitors to each other; in due course, the appendix examines whether this is in fact sufficiently true to make these economies a natural monetary grouping, as the European Monetary System countries are widely agreed to be.

The problem that a common basket peg is intended to address is the instability of the effective exchange rates of the East Asian currencies. As table A2.1 shows, seven of the nine currencies are more unstable in nominal effective terms than in terms of the dollar, and in most cases the instability of the real effective rate is (somewhat) greater still.

One way of curing this problem would be for each of the East Asian economies to peg its currency unilaterally to a trade-weighted basket. But, because the trading patterns of the East Asian economies differ, the cur-

1. The paper was presented at a conference organized by the Association for the Monetary Union of Europe, the Centre d'Etudes Prospectives et d'Informations Internationales, and the Korea Institute of Finance, in Seoul, in December 1996. It is published in Collignon, Pisani-Ferry, and Park (1999). The author gratefully acknowledges the competent research assistance of Molly Mahar. Reprinted with permission from the publisher.

Table A2.1 Relative exchange rate volatility, 1992–95

Economy	Volatility against the dollar	Volatility of the nominal effective exchange rate	Volatility of the real effective exchange rate
China	7.55	7.51	9.58
Hong Kong	0.10	1.01	1.08
Indonesia	0.16	1.29	1.37
Malaysia	1.54	1.67	1.64
The Philippines	2.56	2.71	2.71
Singapore	0.86	1.02	1.13
South Korea	0.58	0.81	0.86
Taiwan	1.45	1.22	1.65
Thailand	0.47	0.86	0.88
Average of 11 floaters[a]	2.71	n.a.	n.a.

n.a. = not available.

a. The 11 floaters are Australia, Canada, Finland, Italy, Japan, New Zealand, Peru, South Africa, Sweden, Switzerland, and the United Kingdom.

Notes: The nominal effective exchange rate is calculated using a trade-weighted average of the national currency value against the dollar, the yen and the deutsche mark. Trade with the Western Hemisphere is included in the dollar weight, and the rest of the world is divided proportionately among the three currencies. Volatility is measured by the standard deviation of changes in end-of-month exchange rates.

Sources: IMF, *International Financial Statistics*; Republic of China, *Financial Statistics*; Williamson (1996, table 8.4).

rency baskets would differ between them. This would mean that a change in the dollar-yen rate would lead to changes in intra-East Asian exchange rates, which is a matter of concern, inasmuch as economies not only have to worry about exporting to and competing with imports from the industrial economies, but also about their markets, their suppliers, and above all their competitors in other East Asian economies. This problem could be addressed through collective action, specifically in the form of the choice of a common peg. The purpose of the appendix is to explore what that would involve.

Consider a simple world where there are only three currencies, the dollar, the yen, and an East Asian currency. For the sake of concreteness, let us take the South Korean won as our example. Suppose that the dollar and the yen are floating against each other. If Korea pegs the won to the dollar, then an appreciation of the yen will lead to an effective depreciation of the won, which will increase Korean competitiveness and thus tend to increase output and strengthen the current account, but will also exert inflationary pressure. If the won had previously been at just the right level to balance the claims of competitiveness against those of inflation control, it will now be too weak. (If, on the contrary, Korea had pegged the won to the yen, then the yen's appreciation would cause the won to be too strong.)

The obvious solution is to replace the dollar by a basket containing both the dollar and the yen, with weights equal to those in the formula for Korea's effective exchange rate. An unchanged peg to that basket will leave the effective exchange rate of the won unchanged, whatever may happen to the yen-dollar rate—changes in which will thus have no impact on Korean output, inflation, or the balance of payments. Korea will have succeeded in insulating itself from the effect of exchange rate fluctuations between the dollar and the yen. Such insulation is, of course, possible only at the macroeconomic level; when the yen appreciates, exporters to Japan will still gain, whereas those who export to the United States will lose.

The real world contains more than three economies, which complicates matters. To some extent, this can be addressed by simply adding extra currencies to the basket. Consider, for example, the trade patterns of the East Asian economies as shown in table A2.2. It is natural to add a European currency, which one would now take to be the euro, to a currency basket for an East Asian currency. The more difficult issues arise in dealing with the weights of the other three groupings: East Asia other than the economy itself, the rest of the Western Hemisphere, and the rest of the world.

Most developing economies in the Western Hemisphere used to peg to the dollar and still tend to focus mainly on the dollar, so the trade weights for these countries can perhaps be added to that for the dollar. The rest of the world, which is a disparate group consisting of countries in the Middle East, the economies in transition, South Asia, Australia and New Zealand, and Africa, is primarily an exporter of primary products. Now, the price of primary products is determined by demand in world markets rather than by supply conditions in the exporting countries, so it would make more sense to distribute the trade shares of those products over the industrial importing countries rather than to include the currencies of the countries that export them. I accordingly assume that the share of the rest of the world should be distributed in proportion to the shares of the Unites States, Japan, Western Europe, and East Asia in gross world product (GWP) to get a correct estimate of the effective exchange rate (and, therefore, to generate an optimal basket).

Constructing an appropriate basket raises other technical issues. First, should one use trade shares (as displayed in table A2.2), or would it not be more appropriate to use as weights the elasticities that measure how trade responds to exchange rate changes? Answer: Elasticity weights are in principle better, but, unless one has some figures that one believes, it is safer to stay with trade weights (Williamson 1982). Second, should one include the nominal exchange rate of a country with such rapid inflation that this will provide erroneous data on the real exchange rate? Answer: Clearly not, although correcting for inflation properly will delay the availability of data so much as to vitiate the object of the exercise, which is to

Table A2.2 Direction of trade of East Asian economies, excluding intragroup trade, in 1994 (percentage)

	China			Hong Kong			Indonesia			South Korea			Malaysia			The Philippines			Singapore			Taiwan			Thailand			Weighted average		
	Ex	Im	Total	Ex	Im	Total	Ex	Im	Total	Ex	Im	Total	Ex	Im	Total	Ex	Im	Total	Ex	Im	Total	Ex	Im	Total	Ex	Im	Total	Ex	Im	Total
United States	28.5	18.0	23.2	40.9	17.9	31.0	24.7	14.7	20.2	30.8	24.9	27.4	36.0	24.3	29.7	50.4	26.0	35.6	35.2	24.1	29.0	55.1	24.8	37.7	35.4	14.9	23.1	36.7	21.4	28.6
Japan	28.6	33.9	31.3	9.8	39.0	22.4	45.4	40.1	43.0	20.3	29.2	27.4	20.3	39.0	30.4	19.7	34.1	28.4	13.2	3.5	7.7	21.1	34.6	28.9	27.5	40.1	35.1	20.8	31.0	26.2
Western Europe	21.2	25.4	23.3	28.2	28.9	28.5	25.8	31.0	28.1	16.9	17.1	17.0	24.7	24.2	24.4	23.2	16.5	19.2	26.5	53.8	41.7	14.3	24.3	20.0	26.9	23.2	24.7	22.7	27.7	25.4
Rest of Western Hemisphere	4.9	5.1	5.0	7.8	2.7	5.6	3.0	4.9	3.8	9.7	5.4	7.3	4.2	2.1	3.0	3.2	3.6	3.4	4.0	2.0	2.9	9.5	3.9	6.3	3.7	2.8	3.1	6.4	3.7	5.0
Rest of world	16.8	17.6	17.2	13.2	11.5	12.5	1.1	9.3	4.8	22.3	23.4	22.9	14.8	1.5	12.5	3.5	19.8	13.4	21.2	16.7	18.7	0.0	12.4	7.1	6.5	19.1	14.1	13.4	16.2	14.9
Deviation from weighted average	23.3	11.4	14.9	22.4	18.4	12.5	55.2	27.3	39.2	24.5	24.6	22.9	6.7	21.8	10.6	28.4	22.6	18.4	23.1	58.5	41.1	43.7	14.4	26.1	21.6	24.0	17.7			

Weights for the common basket	Nine-currency basket	Eight-currency basket	Six-currency basket
US dollar	38.1	39.7	39.3
Japanese yen	32.6	31.0	33.8
Deutsche mark	29.3	29.3	26.8

Ex = exports.

Im = imports.

Note: Figures for Taiwan are a mix of data reported by Taiwan and its trading partners, and are subject to greater than normal error.

Source: IMF, *Direction of Trade Statistics 1995*.

have an index that can guide intervention policy on a real-time basis. However, because most of the high-inflation countries fall into the residual rest-of-the-world category that we have just proposed to redistribute to the industrial countries, this is not in practice a major problem.

One group remains to be dealt with: the other East Asian economies. A unilateral way of dealing with them is to add them also to the basket to which each economy would peg. For example, South Korea would add the currencies of China, Hong Kong, Indonesia, Malaysia, the Philippines, Singapore, Taiwan, and Thailand to the US dollar, the yen, and the euro. This has one advantage: It would stabilize the effective exchange rate, whatever the other East Asian economies did.

But it also has three disadvantages. First, it would make a rather large basket with a long tail of currencies with small weights, and experience has shown that such long tails cause more bother than they are worth, given their very limited impact on the behavior of the basket. Second, several of those economies, notably China and Indonesia, have relatively high inflation, so that it is dangerous to ignore the divergence between nominal and real exchange rates. Third, because the trade structures of the East Asian economies differ significantly, the East Asian currencies would still vary arbitrarily against each other, as a result of the fluctuations among the industrial-country currencies.

An alternative approach would be for each of the East Asian economies to peg its currency to a common basket. Let us assume for the moment that the relevant group of economies does indeed consist of the nine that have been discussed in this paper. To calculate this common basket peg, one would calculate the weighted average of the extra-regional trade of these nine economies, as is done in table A2.2, and then assign the weights of the rest of the Western Hemisphere to the United States and divide that of the rest of the world proportionately to their shares in GWP among the United States, Japan, and Western Europe, as discussed above.

Are the East Asian economies sufficiently important competitors to each other to justify a common monetary arrangement? For each of the nine East Asian economies, table A2.3 lists the eight with the most similar commodity structure of exports (at the 4-digit Standard Industrial Trade Classification, or SITC, level). At the bottom of each column, one can find the number of economies out of the eight closest competitors that are among the eight other East Asian economies being considered. It can be seen that, on average, almost five of each economy's closest eight competitors come from this group. The hypothesis that they are important competitors to one another thus receives ample confirmation.

Table A2.4 compares what would have resulted from following the two alternative strategies outlined above[2] with what actually happened during a period that witnessed a major convulsion in the foreign exchange markets, namely the first 4 months of 1995, when the yen appreciated strongly

---

2. It is assumed here that the euro can be proxied by the deutsche mark.

Table A2.3 Export similarity indices for nine East Asian economies, 1992

China	Hong Kong	Indonesia	South Korea	Malaysia
0.641 Hong Kong	0.641 China	0.400 China	0.540 Hong Kong	0.502 Singapore
0.496 Portugal	0.563 Taiwan	0.375 Tunisia	0.492 Taiwan	0.440 Taiwan
0.471 Thailand	0.540 South Korea	0.373 Norway	0.481 Italy	0.406 South Korea
0.646 South Korea	0.502 Thailand	0.352 Vietnam	0.473 North Korea	0.401 Thailand
0.448 Italy	0.448 Italy	0.338 Malaysia	0.472 Singapore	0.366 Japan
0.437 Yugoslavia	0.462 Portugal	0.332 Thailand	0.471 Japan	0.364 Hong Kong
0.434 Taiwan	0.451 Singapore	0.323 Algeria	0.464 China	0.358 Malta
0.492 Bulgaria	0.410 Austria	0.322 Brunei	0.443 Thailand	0.338 United Kingdom

East Asia in top 8:

4[a]	5	3	5	5

The Philippines	Singapore	Taiwan	Thailand
0.389 Thailand	0.507 Japan	0.563 Hong Kong	0.503 Taiwan
0.328 Australia	0.502 Malaysia	0.503 Thailand	0.502 Hong Kong
0.307 South Korea	0.476 United States	0.492 South Korea	0.471 China
0.305 Malaysia	0.472 South Korea	0.476 Italy	0.443 South Korea
0.302 Hong Kong	0.467 Taiwan	0.467 Singapore	0.425 Singapore
0.301 China	0.451 Hong Kong	0.447 Yugoslavia	0.402 Italy
0.299 Taiwan	0.449 United Kingdom	0.446 Japan	0.401 Malaysia
0.289 Portugal	0.425 Thailand	0.444 Austria	0.389 The Philippines

East Asia in top 8:

6	5	4	7

a. This is the number of economies out of the eight closest competitors that are among the eight other East Asian economies being considered.

Source: From 4-digit SITC codes; Statistics Canada World Trade Dataset.

(by 19.1 percent) against the dollar. Most of the East Asian currencies stuck closely to the dollar (column 1 of the table), and in consequence experienced large depreciations in their effective exchange rates (column 2).

This had implications that were presumptively unfavorable for them, because if their currency were previously at the optimal level (defined as

Table A2.4 Actual and hypothetical exchange rate changes, 31 December 1994 to 30 April 1995

| | Actual rate change | | Hypothetical rate change | | | | | | | |
| | | | Unilateral peg | | 9-currency basket | | 8-currency basket | | 6-currency basket | |
	Against dollar	NEER	Against dollar	NEER	Against dollar	NEER	Against dollar	NEER	Against dollar	NEER
	(1)	(2)	(3)	(4)	(5)	(6)	(7)	(8)	(9)	(10)
China	0.5	-1	7.0	0.0	9.78	-0.86	9.47	-1.16	9.71	-0.92
Hong Kong	-0.1	-7.7	4.7	0.0	9.78	0.94	9.47	0.63	9.71	0.87
Indonesia	3.5	-11.5	12.9	0.0	9.78	-2.44	9.47	0.51[a]	9.71	-2.50[a]
Malaysia	3.6	-5.3	6.5	0.0	9.78	-0.24	9.47	-0.55	9.71	-0.30
The Philippines	-6.2	-13.3	7.1	0.0	9.78	0.83	9.47	0.52	9.71	0.76[a]
Singapore	4.9	-2.9	4.7	0.0	9.78	1.24	9.47	0.93	9.71	1.18[a]
South Korea	-1.2	-4.4	6.9	0.0	9.78	0.81	9.47	0.51	9.71	0.75
Taiwan	3.3	-4.2	6.0	0.0	9.78	1.22	9.47	0.92	9.71	1.16
Thailand	2.1	-7.8	8.2	0.0	9.78	-1.50	9.47	-1.18	9.71	-1.56

Memorandum item: Japan 19.1; Germany 12.0 appreciation against the US dollar.

NEER = Nominal Effective Exchange Rate.

a. Shows the impact of pegging to an East Asian currency basket which excludes the country's own trade pattern.

Note: An increase indicates an appreciation.

that which balances the benefits of greater competitiveness against the cost of more inflationary pressure), then it must have been too weak afterward: Excess inflation pressure must have emerged. Had they pegged unilaterally to a trade-weighted basket, then by definition there would have been no change in their effective exchange rates (column 4 of table A2.4). However, as can be seen from column 3, this would have involved significantly different moves against the dollar, and hence against each other. In contrast, a common basket peg based on the external trade of the nine economies, as constructed in table A2.2 and whose results are shown in columns 5 and 6 of table A2.4, would have resulted in an identical 9.8 percent appreciation against the dollar, but in modestly different changes in the effective exchange rates.

The identical nominal appreciations presuppose that each of the nine economies would have pegged rigidly to the common peg. Because only Hong Kong has a rigid peg these days, this is an improbable assumption. Once one allows for substantial bands around parity, actual outcomes would depend on the workings of the foreign exchange market: An appreciation of the parity would not automatically imply an equal appreciation of the market exchange rate. But, if the band were credible, the central expectation would be for the market exchange rate to stay at the same position within the band, and therefore to appreciate by as much as the parity did. The existence of a common peg would still suffice to create a strong tendency for the East Asian currencies to stick together in the face of common shocks emanating from exchange rate instability in the outside world.

The nine economies on which attention has so far been focused were selected because of an a priori belief that they were important as competitors to one another. It is now time to examine whether this is a logical group to share a common exchange rate peg. Such a common peg would be attractive if two conditions are satisfied.

The first is that the geographical distribution of trade (excluding intra-trade) of the economies is similar. Table A2.2 permits such a comparison. The last row sums the absolute values of the deviations in the trade shares of each economy from the regional average. It suggests that a common peg would be particularly good for China, Hong Kong, and Malaysia; about average for South Korea, the Philippines, Taiwan, and Thailand; but distinctly less satisfactory for Indonesia and Singapore.

The second condition is that the economies are close competitors in world markets. Table A2.3 shows that, with the exception of Indonesia, each of them has at least half its eight principal competitors as other economies of the region. Similarly, each except Indonesia and the Philippines appears as one of the principal competitors of at least four other economies of the region. Other economies that appear as principal competitors more than twice are Italy (5 times), Japan (4 times), and Portugal (3 times). Italy has none of the East Asian economies among its eight principal competitors, Japan has one (Singapore), and Portugal has three (China, Hong Kong, and South Korea). If one sums the number of times that each of our eight economies has, and appears as, a principal competitor of the others, one gets the following result:

Thailand	15
Hong Kong	12
South Korea	12
Taiwan	11
Malaysia	10
Singapore	10
China	9
The Philippines	7
Indonesia	3

Analogous figures for the non-East Asian economies are:

Portugal	6
Italy	5
Japan	5

With the exception of Indonesia, the East Asian economies are unambiguously more important as competitors with each other than with any outside economies.

Taking the two criteria together—the extent to which a common peg would be satisfactory and the similarity in their export patterns—it is clear that Indonesia is a marginal candidate for inclusion in the East Asian group. Singapore is a weak candidate on the first criterion, and the Philippines is somewhat marginal on the second. Hence two additional trade baskets were calculated: one for eight economies (excluding Indonesia), and another for the six core economies (excluding Indonesia, the Philippines, and Singapore).

The final columns of table A2.4 show the impact on the dollar and effective exchange rates of each of the East Asian currencies of a peg to each of those two baskets during the period of dramatic yen appreciation in early 1995. The interesting feature is how little difference it makes to an economy whether its own trade is included in the basket or not. Indeed, Indonesia would have been slightly better off with the six-economy basket than with the nine-economy basket that included its own trade pattern. All of them would still have been vastly better off with the basket than with their actual policy.

It is of course possible that some of the East Asian economies were wanting to increase competitiveness, in which case a common peg would have thwarted what came as a boon to them. But there is another possible explanation for why their appreciations (against the dollar) were weak or nonexistent, which is that they were faced with a classic problem of collective action. Each of them could quite rationally have felt compelled to stay close to the dollar, because they feared that appreciation against the dollar would also have meant appreciation against their regional competitors (as it actually would have done). The solution to this collective action problem is precisely the adoption of a common basket peg. This would provide each of the East Asian economies with some assurance that its competitiveness was not going to be undermined vis-à-vis its peers if it allowed its currency to appreciate against the dollar when the dollar is weak.

To get a summary figure of the relative stability (in terms of effective exchange rates) that would have been yielded by different policies, one can calculate the average absolute value of the changes in nominal effective exchange rates under each of the five policies. These are as follows:

Actual policy	7.4
Unilateral basket pegs	0.0
Nine-currency basket	1.1
Eight-currency basket	1.1
Six-currency basket	1.1

It is evident that the choice between the three baskets is not an issue of much consequence. In contrast, any of the common baskets would have

Table A2.5 Export similarity indices for nine EU countries, 1992

Austria	Belgium and Luxembourg	Denmark	France	Germany
0.633 Germany	0.637 Germany	0.526 The Netherlands	0.723 Germany	0.723 France
0.594 Sweden	0.597 The Netherlands	0.493 Germany	0.674 United Kingdom	0.652 United Kingdom
0.594 Italy	0.592 France	0.481 Italy	0.645 United States	0.645 Spain
0.581 France	0.579 Spain	0.478 France	0.614 Spain	0.642 Italy
0.512 Spain	0.536 United Kingdom	0.463 Belgium-Luxembourg	0.592 Belgium-Luxembourg	0.637 Belgium-Luxembourg
0.512 United Kingdom	0.500 Austria	0.460 United Kingdom	0.589 Italy	0.633 Austria
0.500 United States	0.494 Sweden	0.447 Austria	0.587 The Netherlands	0.631 Japan
0.500 Belgium-Luxembourg	0.492 Italy	0.444 United States	0.581 Austria	0.620 United States

European Union in top 8:

7[a]	6	7	6	6

Italy	The Netherlands	Sweden	United Kingdom
0.642 Germany	0.597 Belgium-Luxembourg	0.610 Germany	0.718 United States
0.594 Austria	0.587 France	0.607 Finland	0.674 France
0.592 Spain	0.578 Germany	0.594 Austria	0.652 Germany
0.589 France	0.565 United States	0.568 France	0.563 The Netherlands
0.544 United	0.563 United Kingdom	0.529 United Kingdom	0.544 Italy
0.530 Yugoslavia	0.562 Denmark	0.525 Spain	0.563 Belgium-Luxembourg
0.516 United States	0.503 Italy	0.524 Canada	0.529 Sweden
0.513 Sweden	0.495 Spain	0.522 United States	0.528 Japan

European Union in top 8:

5	6	4	6

a. This is the number of countries out of the eight closest competitors that are among the eight other EU countries being considered.

Source: From 4-digit SITC codes; Statistics Canada World Trade Dataset.

got on average 85 percent of the benefits of the set of unilateral pegs, even using a measure that attributes zero significance to holding the relative competitiveness of the East Asian economies constant.

The one area of the world that appears to have economies even more competitive with one another than East Asia is Western Europe. Table A2.5

shows export similarity indices for nine core members of the European Union analogous to those for the East Asian economies in table A2.3. This shows that on average the European economies have 5.8 of their top eight competitors among the other eight economies considered, as against an average of 4.9 in East Asia (or 5.1, excluding Indonesia).

Those close trade interrelations long ago led the European countries to adopt a concerted exchange rate policy. The European Monetary System, and specifically its Exchange Rate Mechanism, was created precisely to insulate the European countries from the instabilities that would otherwise have been imposed on Europe by fluctuations in the value of the dollar.

The ERM provided for a mutual pegging mechanism among the participating currencies, with narrow bands (plus or minus 2.25 percent), and requiring unanimous agreement to any parity changes. However, the failure to realign after 1987 led to growing disequilibriums, which in due course fostered the great ERM crises of 1992–93, as a result of which the ERM bands had to be widened to plus or minus 15 percent. The ERM was replaced by a single currency, the euro, for 11 of the core EU countries at the beginning of 1999.

East Asia may also have got to the stage where it could benefit from some concertation in its exchange rate policies, but one may doubt whether it is ready to replicate the ERM. One reason is that the foreign exchange markets of some of the prospective members, especially China, have not yet developed to the point where one would expect effective intervention to defend the cross-rates in other participating economies to be possible (not to mention possible political problems in agreeing on how to defend the margins between the remnimbi and the New Taiwan dollar). Another reason is that the economies still have too wide a range of preferences regarding exchange rate policy, and of inflation rates, to permit adoption of as tight a system as the ERM, with its presumption against frequent parity changes.

The alternative that I have outlined above is adoption of a common basket peg. This would permit Hong Kong to continue to operate a currency board system, if that is what it wishes to do: It would simply start to trade US dollars for Hong Kong dollars at a price that would vary depending on the value of the US dollar in the foreign exchange markets vis-à-vis the other currencies in the basket (plus or minus the margins), instead of at a fixed rate.[3] Both China and Taiwan could intervene in their own markets quite independently of one another, pretending that the other does not exist.

Some economies can operate wide bands if they so wish, whereas others can defend much narrower margins. Some can have their bands crawl, if that is needed to offset differential inflation or to avoid importing infla-

---

3. It could easily diversify its reserve holdings to match the currency basket, or cover its dollar holdings forward to provide similar insurance, if it wished to avoid any foreign exchange exposure.

tion or to facilitate a desired balance of payments adjustment. If the participants want to get together in concert on these policies, they can do so, but it is not essential that they do so.

The object of the change would simply be to create an expectation that, even without any such concertation, variations in the exchange rates among the industrial economies would no longer have major impacts on the relative competitive positions of the East Asian economies. That would be a significant first practical step toward the East Asian monetary cooperation for which leaders in the region have begun to call. It would also have yielded significant benefits during the period 1995–96, inasmuch as one of the reasons for the boom of 1995 and the near-recession of 1996 was the impact on trade flows of the region's effective depreciation early in 1995 and the subsequent appreciation. A basket peg that had kept the region's effective exchange rates roughly constant would have avoided those destabilizing impacts. And, one may add with the benefit of hindsight in 2000, it would have helped to limit the pressures that led to the 1997 crisis, as argued in the main text.

References

Agosin, Manuel R. 1995. El Retorno de los Capitales Extranjeros Privados a Chile. *El Trimestre Económico* 62, no. 4 (October–December): 467–94.

Agosin, Manuel R. 1998. Capital Inflow and Investment Performance: Chile in the 1980s. In *Capital Inflows and Investment Performance: Lessons from Latin America*, eds. R. Ffrench-Davis and H. Reisen. Paris: OECD Development Centre; and Santiago: ECLAC.

Agosin, Manuel R., and Ricardo Ffrench-Davis. 1999. Managing Capital Inflows in Chile. In *Short-term Capital Flows and Economic Crises*, eds. S. Griffith-Jones, M.F. Montes, and A. Nasution. New York: Oxford University Press for World Institute for Development Economics Research.

Alesina, Alberto, Vittorio Grilli, and Gian Maria Milesi-Ferretti. 1994. The Political Economy of Capital Controls. In *Capital Mobility: The Impact on Consumption and Growth*, eds. L. Leiderman and A. Razin. Cambridge: Cambridge University Press.

Ariyoshi, Akira, Karl Habermeier, Bernard Laurens, Inci Otker-Robe, Jorge Ivan Canales-Kriljenko, and Andrei Kirilenko. 2000. *Country Experiences with the Use and Liberalization of Capital Controls.* Washington: International Monetary Fund.

Balassa, Bela. 1964. The Purchasing Power Parity Doctrine: A Reappraisal. *Journal of Political Economy* 72, no. 6 (December): 584–6

Balassa, Bela, and John Williamson. 1987. *Adjusting to Success: Balance of Payments Policy in the East Asian NICs.* Washington: Institute for International Economics.

Bartolini, Leonardo, and Allan Drazen. 1997. Capital Account Liberalization as a Signal. *American Economic Review* 87, no. 1 (March): 138–54.

Bartolini, Leonardo, and Alessandro Prati. 1997. Soft versus Hard Targets for Intervention. *Economic Policy*, no. 24 (April): 14–52.

Bartolini, Leonardo, and Alessandro Prati. 1998. *Soft Exchange Rate Bands and Speculative Attacks: Theory, and Evidence from the ERM since August 1993.* IMF Working Paper 98/156. Washington: International Monetary Fund.

Bergsten, C. Fred, and John Williamson. 1983. Exchange Rates and Trade Policy. In *Trade Policy in the 1980s*, ed. W.R. Cline. Washington: Institute for International Economics.

Bhagwati, Jagdish N. 1998. The Capital Myth. *Foreign Affairs* 77, no. 3 (May–June): 7–12.

Bofinger, Peter. 1999. *Options for the Exchange Rate Management of the European Central Bank.* European Parliament Working Paper ECON 115 EN. Luxembourg: European Parliament.

Calvo, Guillermo A., and Carmen M. Reinhart. 2000. *Fear of Floating*. Photocopy. College Park, MD: University of Maryland.

Catte, Pietro, Giampaolo Galli, and Salvatore Rebecchini. 1994. Concerted Interventions and the Dollar: An Analysis of Daily Data. In *The International Monetary System*, eds. P.B. Kenen, F. Papadia, and F. Saccomanni. Cambridge: Cambridge University Press.

Chan, K.C. 1999. The Hong Kong Currency Board: Crisis, Reform, and Future Prospects. Paper presented at a conference on exchange rate regimes in emerging-market economies, sponsored by the Asian Development Bank Institute, Centre d'Etudes Prospectives et d'Informations Internationales, and Korean Institute for International Economic Policy, Tokyo (17–18 December).

Collignon, Stefan, Jean Pisani-Ferry, and Yung Chul Park. 1999. *Exchange Rate Policies in Emerging Asian Countries*. New York: Routledge.

Cooper, Richard N. 1999. Should Capital Controls Be Banished? *Brookings Papers on Economic Activity 1*: 89–125. Washington: Brookings Institution.

Crockett, Andrew. 1994. Monetary Implications of Increased Capital Flows. In *Changing Capital Markets: Implications for Policy*, ed. Federal Reserve Bank of Kansas City. Kansas City: Federal Reserve Bank of Kansas City.

De Gregorio, Jose, Sebastian Edwards, and Rodrigo O. Valdes. 2000. *Controls on Capital Inflows: Do they Work? Working Paper*, UCLA Anderson School of Business (January). Photocopy. Forthcoming in the *Journal of Development Economics*.

Dominguez, Kathryn M., and Jeffrey A. Frankel. 1993. *Does Foreign Exchange Intervention Work?* Washington: Institute for International Economics.

Dornbusch, Rudiger, and Yung Chul Park. 1999. Flexibility or nominal anchors? In *Exchange Rate Policies in Emerging Asian Countries*, eds. S. Colligan, J. Pisani-Ferry, and Y.C. Park. New York: Routledge.

Edwards, Sebastian. 1999a. *On Crisis Prevention: Lessons from Mexico and East Asia*. NBER Working Paper 7233. Cambridge, MA: National Bureau of Economic Research.

Eichengreen, Barry. 1994. *International Monetary Arrangements for the 21st Century*. Washington: Brookings Institution.

Ethier, Wilfred, and Arthur I. Bloomfield. 1975. *Managing the Managed Float*. Princeton Essays in International Finance 112. Princeton, NJ: Princeton University Press.

Fischer, Bernard, and Helmut Reisen. 1992. *Towards Capital Account Convertibility*. Policy Brief 4. Paris: OECD Development Centre.

Fischer, Stanley. 1999. Concluding remarks at a conference on key issues in reform of the international monetary and financial system, sponsored by the IMF, Washington (28–29 May).

Frankel, Jeffrey A. 1999. *No Single Currency Regime Is Right for All Countries or at All Times*. Princeton Essays in International Finance 215. Princeton, NJ: Princeton University Press.

Friedman, Milton. 1953. The Case for Flexible Exchange Rates. In *Essays in Positive Economics*, ed. Milton Friedman. Chicago: University of Chicago Press.

Gallego, Francisco, Leonardo Hernandez, and Klaus Schmidt-Hebel. 1999. Capital Controls in Chile: Effective? Efficient? Paper presented at a conference on capital flows, financial crises, and policies, sponsored by the World Bank, Washington (15–16 April).

Goldstein, Morris. 1995. *The Exchange Rate System and the IMF: A Modest Agenda*. Washington: Institute for International Economics.

Goldstein, Morris, Graciela Kaminsky, and Carmen Reinhart. 2000. *Assessing Financial Vulnerability: An Early Warning System for Emerging Markets*. Washington: Institute for International Economics.

Goodhart, Charles, and P.J.R. Delargy. 1998. Financial Crises: Plus ça change, plus c'est la même chose. *International Finance 1*, no. 2: 261–87.

Gros, Daniel, and Niels Thygesen. 1992. *European Monetary Integration*. London: Longman.

Herrera, Luis Oscar, and Rodrigo Valdes. 1999. *The Effect of Capital Controls on Interest Rate Differentials*. Working Paper 50. Santiago: Central Bank of Chile.

Hinkle, Lawrence E., and Peter J. Montiel. 1999. *Exchange Rate Misalignment: Concepts and Measurement for Developing Countries*. New York: Oxford University Press for the World Bank.

Isard, Peter, and Michael Mussa. 1998. A Methodology for Exchange Rate Assessment. In *Exchange Rate Assessment: Extensions of the Macroeconomic Balance Approach*, eds. P. Isard and H. Faruqee. Washington: International Monetary Fund.

Jeanne, Olivier, and Andrew Rose. 1999. *Noise Trading and Exchange Rate Regimes*. NBER Working Paper no. W7104 (April). Photocopy. Cambridge, MA: National Bureau of Economic Research.

Jurgensen Report. 1983. *Report of the Working Group on Exchange Market Intervention*. Washington: US Treasury.

Krugman, Paul. 1979. A Model of Balance-of-Payments Crises. *Journal of Money, Credit, and Banking* 11, no. 3: 311–24.

Krugman, Paul. 1991. Target Zones and Exchange Rate Dynamics. *Quarterly Journal of Economics* 106, no. 3 (August): 669–82.

Krugman, Paul, and Marcus Miller. 1993. Why Have a Target Zone? *Carnegie-Rochester Series on Public Policy* 38: 279–314.

Kwan, C.H. 1998. The Yen, the Yuan, and the Asian Currency Crisis: Changing Fortune between Japan and China. Photocopy (October). Tokyo: Nomura Research Institute.

Labán, Raúl, and Felipe Larraín. 1997. Can a Liberalization of Capital Outflows Increase Net Capital Inflows? *Journal of International Money and Finance* 16, no. 3 (June): 415–31.

Larraín, F., Raúl Labán, and R. Chumacero. 1997. What Determines Capital Inflows? An Empirical Analysis for Chile. Faculty Research Working Paper Series R97-18, Photocopy. Cambridge, MA: John F. Kennedy School of Government, Harvard University.

Laurens, Bernard, and Jaime Cardoso. 1998. *Managing Capital Flows: Lessons from the Experience of Chile*. IMF Working Paper 98/168. Washington: International Monetary Fund.

Le Fort, Guillermo, and Sergio Lehmann. 2000. El Encaje, Los Flujos de Capitales y el Gasto: Una Evaluacion Empirica. *Documentos de Trabajo*, no. 64. Santiago: Central Bank of Chile.

Masson, Paul. 2000. Exchange Rate Regime Transitions. Photocopy. Washington: Brookings Institution.

Masson, Paul, E. Jadresic, and P. Mauro. 1999. The Choice of an Exchange Rate Regime Revisited. Paper presented at a conference on exchange rate regimes in emerging-market economies, sponsored by the Asian Development Bank Institute, Centre d'Etudes Prospectives et d'Informations Internationales, and Korean Institute for International Economic Policy, Tokyo (17–18 December).

McKinnon, Ronald I. 2000. The East Asian Dollar Standard: Life After Death? *Economic Notes* 29, no. 1: 31–82.

Meese, Richard, and Kenneth Rogoff. 1983. Empirical Exchange Rate Models of the 1970s: Do They Fit Out of Sample? *Journal of International Economics* 14, no. 1–2 (February): 3–24.

Mussa, Michael, Paul Masson, Alexander Swoboda, Esteban Jadresic, Paolo Mauro, and Andy Berg. 2000. *Exchange Rate Regimes in an Increasingly Integrated World Economy*. Washington: International Monetary Fund.

Nadal-De Simone, Francisco, and Piritta Sorsa. 1999. *A Review of Capital Account Restrictions in Chile in the 1990s*. IMF Working Paper 99/52. Washington: International Monetary Fund.

Obstfeld, Maurice. 1986. Rational and Self-Fulfilling Balance-of-Payments Crises. *American Economic Review* 76, no. 1 (March): 72–81.

Obstfeld, Maurice, and Kenneth Rogoff. 1995. The Mirage of Fixed Exchange Rates. *Journal of Economic Perspectives* 9, no. 4: 73–96.

Ogawa, Eiji, and Takatoshi Ito. 1999. On the Desirability of a Regional Basket Currency Arrangement. Paper presented at a conference sponsored by Asian Development Bank Institute, Centre d'Etudes Prospectives et d'Informations Internationales, and Korean Institute for International Economic Policy, Tokyo (17–18 December).

Ohno, Kenichi, Kazuko Shirono, and Elif Sisli. 1999. Can High Interest Rates Stop Regional Currency Crises? Photocopy. Tokyo: Asian Development Bank Institute.

Ortiz, Guillermo, and Agustin Carstens. 2000. The Experience with a Floating Exchange Rate Regime: The Case of Mexico. Paper presented at a conference on international financial markets: the challenge of globalization, Texas A&M University, College Station (31 March).

Park, Yung Chul, Yunjong Wang, and Chae-Shick Chung. 1999. Exchange Rate Policies in Korea: Has Exchange Rate Volatility Increased after the Crisis? Paper presented at a conference on exchange rate policies in emerging-market economies, sponsored by Asian Development Bank Institute, Centre d'Etudes Prospectives et d'Informations Internationales, and Korean Institute for International Economic Policy, Tokyo (17–18 December).

Pisani-Ferry, Jean, and Benoit Coeure. 1999. The Exchange-Rate Regime Among Major Currencies. Paper presented at a conference on key issues in the reform of the international monetary and financial system, sponsored by the IMF, Washington (28–29 May).

Preeg, Ernest H. 2000. *The Trade Deficit, The Dollar, and the U.S. National Interest.* Indianapolis: Hudson Institute.

Quinn, Dennis. 1997. The Correlates of Changes in International Financial Regulation. *American Political Science Review* 91, no. 3: 531–51.

Reisen, Helmut, and Isabelle Journard. 1992. Real Exchange Rate Overshooting and Persistent Trade Effects: The Case of New Zealand. *The World Economy* 15, no. 3 (May): 375–88.

Reisen, Helmut, and Axel van Trotsenburg. 1988. Should the Asian NICs Peg to the Yen? *Intereconomics*, July–August: 172–77.

Rodrik, Dani. 1998. Who Needs Capital Account Convertibility? In *Should the IMF Pursue Capital Account Convertibility?* eds. S. Fischer, R.N. Cooper, R. Dornbusch, P.M. Garber, C. Massad, J.J. Polak, D. Rodrik, and S.S. Tarapore. Princeton Essays in International Finance 207. Princeton, NJ: Princeton University Press.

Rogoff, Kenneth. 1996. The Purchasing Power Parity Puzzle. *Journal of Economic Literature* 34, no. 2 (June): 647–68.

Rose, Andrew. 1996. Exchange Rate Volatility, Monetary Policy, and Capital Mobility: Empirical Evidence on the Holy Trinity. *Journal of International Money and Finance* 15, no. 6: 561–86.

Samuelson, Paul A. 1964. Theoretical Notes on Trade Problems. *Review of Economics and Statistics* 46, no. 2(May): 145–54.

Schulstad, Paul, and Angel Serrat. 1995. An Empirical Examination of a Multilateral Target Zone Model. Documento de Trabajo no. 9532. Madrid: Banco de Espana.

Shiller, Robert J. 2000. *Irrational Exuberance.* Princeton, NJ: Princeton University Press.

Stein, Jerome L., Polly R. Allen, and associates. 1995. *Fundamental Determinants of Exchange Rates.* Oxford: Clarendon Press.

Svensson, Lars E.O. 1992. An Interpretation of Recent Research on Exchange Rate Target Zones. *Journal of Economic Perspectives* 6, no. 4 (Fall): 119–44.

Swoboda, Alexander. 1986. Credibility and Viability in International Monetary Arrangements. *Finance and Development* 23 (September): 15–18.

Tarapore Committee. 1997. *Report of the Committee on Capital Account Convertibility.* Mumbai: Reserve Bank of India.

Uribe, José Dario. 1995. Flujos de Capital en Colombia, 1978–1994. *Revista del Banco de la Republica*, no. 807 (January).

Valdes-Prieto, Salvador, and Marcelo Soto. 1998. The Effectiveness of Capital Controls: Theory and Evidence from Chile. *Empirica* 25: 134–64.

Volcker, Paul. 1978. The Political Economy of the Dollar. Fred Hirsch Memorial Lecture, 9 November. *FRBNY Quarterly Review* (Winter 1978–79): 1–12.

Williamson, John. 1965. *The Crawling Peg.* Princeton Essays in International Finance 50. Princeton, NJ: Princeton University Press.

Williamson, John. 1982. A Survey of the Literature on the Optimal Peg. *Journal of Development Economics* 11 (August): 39–61. [Reprinted in *Political Economy and International Money: Selected Essays of John Williamson*, ed. C. Milner. Brighton: Wheatsheaf, 1987.]

Williamson, John. 1983, 1985. *The Exchange Rate System*, 1st ed., 1983; revised ed., 1985. Washington: Institute for International Economics.

Williamson, John. 1994. *Estimating Equilibrium Exchange Rates*. Washington: Institute for International Economics.

Williamson, John. 1996. *The Crawling Band as an Exchange Rate Regime: Lessons from Chile, Colombia, and Israel*. Washington: Institute for International Economics.

Williamson, John. (1999a), Are Intermediate Regimes Vanishing? Keynote speech given at a conference on exchange rate regimes in emerging-market economies, sponsored by Asian Development Bank Institute, Centre d'Etudes Prospectives et d'Informations Internationales, and Korean Institute for International Economic Policy, Tokyo (17–18 December). http://www.iie.com/staff/willguid.htm.

Williamson, John. 1999b. The Case for a Common Basket Peg for East Asian Currencies. In *Exchange Rate Policies in Emerging Asian Countries*, eds. S. Collignon, J. Pisani-Ferry, and Y.C. Park. London and New York: Routledge.

Williamson, John, and Marcus Miller. 1987. *Targets and Indicators: A Blueprint for the International Coordination of Economic Policy*. Washington: Institute for International Economics.

Wonnacott, Paul. 1965. *The Canadian Dollar, 1948–62*. Toronto: University of Toronto Press.

Wyplosz, Charles. 1998. Currency Crisis Contagion and Containment: A Framework. Paper presented at a conference on financial crises and Asia, sponsored by the Centre for Economic Policy Research, London (4–5 February).

Zee, Howell H. 1999. Retarding Short-Term Capital Inflows through a Withholding Tax. Photocopy. Washington: International Monetary Fund.

Index

China—*continued*
  relative rate volatility, 61, 62t
  trade patterns, 64t, 66t, 68
clean floating. *See* floating, fearless (clean)
Colombia, 9, 11–12, 12, 34
commercial bank, reserve ratio requirement,
    variation of, 35–36
common basket peg, 8n, 8–9, 25, 61–72
  choice of, 69–70
  conditions for, 68–69
  creation of, 63–65, 64t
  crisis-proofing of, 25
  and effective exchange rate, 63, 67, 67t, 69
  European (*See* Exchange Rate Mechanism
    (ERM))
  versus single-currency pegs, 8–9, 11n
  and trade patterns, 63–68, 64t, 66t
  and yen-dollar exchange rate, 8–9, 62, 64t, 65,
    69
competition, trade, and common basket peg, 65,
    66t, 68–69
competitive rate
  and common peg, 62–63
  maintenance of, 20–21
cooperative sterilized intervention, 2, 35
corners, vulnerability to crisis, 15–17
corporate sector borrowing, Indonesia, 40
crawl, 9, 25
crawling bands, 6, 9, 11–12. *See also* target zones
  announcement of, 49
  management of, 12
  objectives of, 21–23
  with soft margins, 29
  unannounced, 48–49
  vulnerability to crisis, 29
credibility of authorities, 30, 50, 56
crisis problem, 5–13
crisis resolution, process of, 28
cross-border capital tax, 45
currency board, 16, 31–33
  abandonment of, 15–17
  public confidence in, 16
current account transactions, liberalization of, 36

deflation, 18, 18n
devaluations, 5–6
  inadvertent, avoidance of, 8
  and misalignments, 18, 18n
  disintermediation, 36
dollar-euro target zone, 35
dollar misalignments, 18
dollar peg, 8–9
  BBC rules *versus*, 10
  versus currency baskets, 8–9, 11n
dollar-yen peg, for common basket, 8–9, 9n, 62,
    64t, 65, 69
domestic stabilization, role of monetary policy in,
    32n, 32–33
Dornbusch, Rudiger, 6
Dow Jones Industrial Average, 16

economic growth, high, management
    requirements during, 21, 22t
economic performance, effect of misalignments
    on, 19–20, 56
effective exchange rate, 8n
  and basket calculation, 63, 67, 67t, 69
  instability of, 61, 62t
  real, 8n, 9
    neutral, 28
elasticity weights, and basket construction, 63–65,
    64t
equilibrium exchange rate, 26
  estimated, announcement of, 28–30
  fundamental, 6–7, 18, 26, 36
  market ignorance of, 29–30
equilibrium interest differential, 41–42
euro
  and common basket peg, 63, 64t, 65, 65n, 71
  misalignments, 17–18
euro-dollar target zone, 35
European Monetary System, 61, 71
European Union (EU)
  export similarity indices, 70t, 70–71
  soft margins, 26n
Exchange Rate Mechanism (ERM), 7, 12–13, 23n,
    27, 71
export growth, and crawling bands, 12
export similarity indices
  East Asia, 65, 66t
  European Union, 70t, 70–71

FDI. *See* foreign direct investment (FDI)
FEER. *See* fundamental equilibrium exchange rate
    (FEER)
financial institutions, government-controlled,
    management of, 36
financial solvency, 18
fiscal policy, tightening of, 36–37
"fixed but adjustable-under-market-pressure"
    peg, 48, 50
fixed rate
  versus flexible rates, traditional analysis of, 54–55
  misalignments under, 18
  volatility of, 57–59, 58t
floating, 57–59
  advantages of, 53
  versus bands, 23
  Chile, 12
  Colombia, 12
  drawbacks of, 55–56
  fearless (clean), 13, 57–59
  fear of, 2, 12, 20, 21, 28, 50, 53, 57–59
  versus fixed rate, traditional analysis of, 54–55
  IMF guidelines for, 26, 26n
  India, 19–20
  managed (*See* managed floating)
  misalignment with, 17–18
  New Zealand, 19–20
  volatility measures, 57–59, 58t
  vulnerability to crisis, 17

foreign debt
  burden of, 28
  real value of, 18
foreign direct investment (FDI), liberalization of,
    36–39
forward rate, 23, 55
free markets, ideological faith in, 17–18
fundamental equilibrium exchange rate (FEER),
    6–7, 18, 26, 36

GDP growth, high, management requirements
    during, 21, 22t
George, Henry, 41
Germany, 33n
gold standard, 28
government-controlled financial institutions,
    management of, 36
grants to direct investors, 37
gross world product (GWP), 63, 65
Group of Seven (G-7), 53
Group of Twenty, 1

hedging, 5
Hong Kong, 8, 16, 16n, 47
  and common basket peg, 61–72
  growth rate, 21, 22n
  rate changes, 67t
  relative rate volatility, 61, 62t
  trade patterns, 64t, 66t, 68
Hong Kong Monetary Authority, 16

Ibrahim, Anwar, 39
IMF. *See* International Monetary Fund (IMF)
import restrictions, reduction of, 36
India
  capital account convertibility, 28, 28n
  growth rate, 21, 22n
  misalignments, 19–20, 20n
  volatility measures, 57–59, 58t
Indonesia, 8, 8n, 18, 25
  and common basket peg, 61–72
  corporate sector borrowing, 40
  crisis model, 11
  growth rate, 21, 22n
  rate changes, 67t
  relative rate volatility, 61, 62t
  trade patterns, 64t, 66t, 68
inflation
  and common basket peg, 62–65
  and crawling bands, 12
  differential, neutralization of, 9
  and misalignments, 18, 18n
insurance, of bank deposits, 37
interest rates
  effect of capital controls on, 41–42
  effect on exchange rates, 31–33
  raising of, by run on currency, 16
  reduction of, 36–37
intermediate regimes
  comparison of, 29–30

crisis-proofing of, 25–30
end of, 15–24
versus managed floating, 47–48, 51
positive side of, 17–18
vulnerability to attack, 29–30
International Monetary Fund (IMF), 1
  capital controls policy, 38, 38n
  exchange rate estimates, 6
  Guidelines for Floating, 26
  intermediate techniques advocacy, 56
  pressure to float from, 53
investment
  foreign direct, liberalization of, 36–39
  incentive for, and misalignments, 18
investment decisions, and parity, 7
investors, direct, grants to, 37
Israel, 9, 11–13, 13n

Japan, 32, 57–59, 58t
Jurgensen Report, 34

Korea. *See* South Korea

Latin America, 2. *See also specific country*
"leaning against the wind," 48n, 48–49
liberalization
  of capital accounts, 38–39
  of capital outflows, 36
  of current account transactions, 36
  of foreign direct investment, 36–39
  microeconomic, and misalignments, 19–20
low-income countries, isolation from capital
    market, 15

macroeconomic policy stance, and misalignments,
    20, 24
Malaysia, 47
  capital controls, 39
  and common basket peg, 61–72
  rate changes, 67t
  relative rate volatility, 61, 62t
  trade patterns, 64t, 66t, 68
  volatility measures, 57–59, 58t
managed floating, 6, 13, 47–51
  alternative strategies, 48–49
  definition of, 47
  disadvantages of, 50–51, 53
  versus formal intermediate regimes, 47–48, 51
  versus monitoring bands, 51
  volatility and, 58n, 58–59
market operators, ignorance of equilibrium
    exchange rate, 29–30
Mexico, 11, 12, 57–59, 58t, 59n
microeconomic liberalization, and misalignments,
    19–20
misalignments
  avoidance of, 20–24, 29–30
  and crawling bands, 21–23
  definition of, 18
  effect on economic performance, 19–20, 56

Taiwan
and common basket peg, 61–72
growth rate, 21, 22n
rate changes, 67t
relative rate volatility, 61, 62t
trade patterns, 64t, 66t, 68
Tarapore, S.S., 28
target zones, 6, 23n, 23–24
monetary policy to defend, 32–33
soft, 26n–27n, 26–28
sterilized intervention, 33–35
vulnerability to crisis, 29
tax
capital, cross-border, 45
Tobin, 38n
tax holidays, 37
Thailand
and common basket peg, 61–72
crisis model, 10–11, 10n–11n
rate changes, 67t
real effective exchange rate, 9
relative rate volatility, 61, 62t
trade patterns, 64t, 66t, 68
volatility measures, 57–59, 58t
Tobin tax, 38n
trade competition, and common basket peg, 65,
66t, 68–69
trade patterns
and common basket peg, 63–68, 64t, 66t
European Union, 70t, 70–71
traders
noise, 24

rate forecasts by, and sterilized intervention, 34
stop-loss, 24
transition matrix, 2
transparency, 3, 50–51, 53
Turkey, 11
growth rate, 21, 22n
volatility measures, 57–59, 58t
two corners position, 51

Uganda
growth rate, 21, 22n
volatility measures, 57–59, 58t
unemployment, 18
United States
Treasury Department, 1, 26
volatility measures, 57–59, 58t
unremunerated reserve requirement (URR),
40–45

Venezuela, 9
volatility
fixed rate *versus* floating, 57–59, 58t
relative, 61, 62n

wide bands, 13
definition of, 7
purposes of, 32
versus soft margins, 27

yen-dollar peg, for common basket, 8–9, 9n, 62,
64t, 65, 69
yen misalignments, 18

Other Publications from the Institute for International Economics

* = out of print

POLICY ANALYSES IN INTERNATIONAL ECONOMICS Series

1 The Lending Policies of the International Monetary Fund*   John Williamson
August 1982   ISBN 0-88132-000-5

2 "Reciprocity": A New Approach to World Trade Policy?*   William R. Cline
September 1982   ISBN 0-88132-001-3

3 Trade Policy in the 1980s*
C. Fred Bergsten and William R. Cline
November 1982   ISBN 0-88132-002-1

4 International Debt and the Stability of the World Economy*   William R. Cline
September 1983   ISBN 0-88132-010-2

5 The Exchange Rate System*, Second Edition
John Williamson
Sept. 1983, rev. June 1985 ISBN 0-88132-034-X

6 Economic Sanctions in Support of Foreign Policy Goals*
Gary Clyde Hufbauer and Jeffrey J. Schott
October 1983   ISBN 0-88132-014-5

7 A New SDR Allocation?*   John Williamson
March 1984   ISBN 0-88132-028-5

8 An International Standard for Monetary Stabilization*   Ronald L. McKinnon
March 1984   ISBN 0-88132-018-8

9 The YEN/Dollar Agreement: Liberalizing Japanese Capital Markets* Jeffrey A. Frankel
December 1984   ISBN 0-88132-035-8

10 Bank Lending to Developing Countries: The Policy Alternatives*   C. Fred Bergsten, William R. Cline, and John Williamson
April 1985   ISBN 0-88132-032-3

11 Trading for Growth: The Next Round of Trade Negotiations*
Gary Clyde Hufbauer and Jeffrey R. Schott
September 1985   ISBN 0-88132-033-1

12 Financial Intermediation Beyond the Debt Crisis*   Donald R. Lessard, John Williamson
September 1985   ISBN 0-88132-021-8

13 The United States-Japan Economic Problem*
C. Fred Bergsten and William R. Cline
October 1985, 2d ed. January 1987
                        ISBN 0-88132-060-9

14 Deficits and the Dollar: The World Economy at Risk*   Stephen Marris
December 1985, 2d ed. November 1987
                        ISBN 0-88132-067-6

15 Trade Policy for Troubled Industries*
Gary Clyde Hufbauer and Howard R. Rosen
March 1986   ISBN 0-88132-020-X

16 The United States and Canada: The Quest for Free Trade*   Paul Wonnacott, with an Appendix by John Williamson
March 1987   ISBN 0-88132-056-0

17 Adjusting to Success: Balance of Payments Policy in the East Asian NICs*
Bela Balassa and John Williamson
June 1987, rev. April 1990 ISBN 0-88132-101-X

18 Mobilizing Bank Lending to Debtor Countries*   William R. Cline
June 1987   ISBN 0-88132-062-5

19 Auction Quotas and United States Trade Policy*   C. Fred Bergsten, Kimberly Ann Elliott, Jeffrey J. Schott, and Wendy E. Takacs
September 1987   ISBN 0-88132-050-1

20 Agriculture and the GATT: Rewriting the Rules*   Dale E. Hathaway
September 1987   ISBN 0-88132-052-8

21 Anti-Protection: Changing Forces in United States Trade Politics*
I. M. Destler and John S. Odell
September 1987   ISBN 0-88132-043-9

22 Targets and Indicators: A Blueprint for the International Coordination of Economic Policy* John Williamson and Marcus H. Miller
September 1987   ISBN 0-88132-051-X

23 Capital Flight: The Problem and Policy Responses*   Donald R. Lessard and John Williamson
December 1987   ISBN 0-88132-059-5

24 United States-Canada Free Trade: An Evaluation of the Agreement*
Jeffrey J. Schott
April 1988   ISBN 0-88132-072-2

25 Voluntary Approaches to Debt Relief*
John Williamson
Sept.1988, rev. May 1989 ISBN 0-88132-098-6

26 American Trade Adjustment: The Global Impact*   William R. Cline
March 1989   ISBN 0-88132-095-1

27 More Free Trade Areas?* Jeffrey J. Schott
May 1989   ISBN 0-88132-085-4

28 The Progress of Policy Reform in Latin America*   John Williamson
January 1990   ISBN 0-88132-100-1

29 The Global Trade Negotiations: What Can Be Achieved?*   Jeffrey J. Schott
September 1990   ISBN 0-88132-137-0

30 Economic Policy Coordination: Requiem or Prologue?*   Wendy Dobson
April 1991   ISBN 0-88132-102-8

Trade Protection in the United States: 31 Case Studies*   Gary Clyde Hufbauer, Diane E. Berliner, and Kimberly Ann Elliott
1986   ISBN 0-88132-040-4
Toward Renewed Economic Growth in Latin America*   Bela Balassa, Gerardo M. Bueno, Pedro-Pablo Kuczynski, and Mario Henrique Simonsen
1986   ISBN 0-88132-045-5
Capital Flight and Third World Debt*
Donald R. Lessard and John Williamson, editors
1987   ISBN 0-88132-053-6
The Canada-United States Free Trade Agreement: The Global Impact*
Jeffrey J. Schott and Murray G. Smith, editors
1988   ISBN 0-88132-073-0
World Agricultural Trade: Building a Consensus*
William M. Miner and Dale E. Hathaway, editors
1988   ISBN 0-88132-071-3
Japan in the World Economy*
Bela Balassa and Marcus Noland
1988   ISBN 0-88132-041-2
America in the World Economy: A Strategy for the 1990s   C. Fred Bergsten
1988   ISBN 0-88132-089-7
Managing the Dollar: From the Plaza to the Louvre*   Yoichi Funabashi
1988, 2d ed. 1989   ISBN 0-88132-097-8
United States External Adjustment and the World Economy*   William R. Cline
May 1989   ISBN 0-88132-048-X
Free Trade Areas and U.S. Trade Policy*
Jeffrey J. Schott, editor
May 1989   ISBN 0-88132-094-3
Dollar Politics: Exchange Rate Policymaking in the United States*
I.M. Destler and C. Randall Henning
September 1989   ISBN 0-88132-079-X
Latin American Adjustment: How Much Has Happened?*   John Williamson, editor
April 1990   ISBN 0-88132-125-7
The Future of World Trade in Textiles and Apparel*   William R. Cline
1987, 2d ed. June 1990 ISBN 0-88132-110-9
Completing the Uruguay Round: A Results-Oriented Approach to the GATT Trade Negotiations*   Jeffrey J. Schott, editor
September 1990   ISBN 0-88132-130-3
Economic Sanctions Reconsidered (2 volumes)
Economic Sanctions Reconsidered: Supplemental Case Histories
Gary Clyde Hufbauer, Jeffrey J. Schott, and Kimberly Ann Elliott
1985, 2d ed. Dec. 1990 ISBN cloth 0-88132-115-X
                          ISBN paper 0-88132-105-2

Economic Sanctions Reconsidered: History and Current Policy
Gary Clyde Hufbauer, Jeffrey J. Schott, and Kimberly Ann Elliott
December 1990   ISBN cloth 0-88132-140-0
                          ISBN paper 0-88132-136-2
Pacific Basin Developing Countries: Prospects for the Future*   Marcus Noland
January 1991   ISBN cloth 0-88132-141-9
                          ISBN 0-88132-081-1
Currency Convertibility in Eastern Europe*
John Williamson, editor
October 1991   ISBN 0-88132-128-1
International Adjustment and Financing: The Lessons of 1985-1991*   C. Fred Bergsten, editor
January 1992   ISBN 0-88132-112-5
North American Free Trade: Issues and Recommendations
Gary Clyde Hufbauer and Jeffrey J. Schott
April 1992   ISBN 0-88132-120-6
Narrowing the U.S. Current Account Deficit*
Allen J. Lenz
June 1992   ISBN 0-88132-103-6
The Economics of Global Warming
William R. Cline/*June 1992*   ISBN 0-88132-132-X
U.S. Taxation of International Income: Blueprint for Reform*   Gary Clyde Hufbauer, assisted by Joanna M. van Rooij
October 1992   ISBN 0-88132-134-6
Who's Bashing Whom? Trade Conflict in High-Technology Industries   Laura D'Andrea Tyson
November 1992   ISBN 0-88132-106-0
Korea in the World Economy   Il SaKong
January 1993   ISBN 0-88132-183-4
Pacific Dynamism and the International Economic System*
C. Fred Bergsten and Marcus Noland, editors
May 1993   ISBN 0-88132-196-6
Economic Consequences of Soviet Disintegration*
John Williamson, editor
May 1993   ISBN 0-88132-190-7
Reconcilable Differences? United States-Japan Economic Conflict
C. Fred Bergsten and Marcus Noland
June 1993   ISBN 0-88132-129-X
Does Foreign Exchange Intervention Work?
Kathryn M. Dominguez and Jeffrey A. Frankel
September 1993   ISBN 0-88132-104-4
Sizing Up U.S. Export Disincentives*
J. David Richardson
September 1993   ISBN 0-88132-107-9
NAFTA: An Assessment
Gary Clyde Hufbauer and Jeffrey J. Schott/*rev. ed.*
October 1993   ISBN 0-88132-199-0

Adjusting to Volatile Energy Prices
Philip K. Verleger, Jr.
November 1993   ISBN 0-88132-069-2

The Political Economy of Policy Reform
John Williamson, editor
January 1994   ISBN 0-88132-195-8

Measuring the Costs of Protection
in the United States
Gary Clyde Hufbauer and Kimberly Ann Elliott
January 1994   ISBN 0-88132-108-7

The Dynamics of Korean Economic Development
Cho Soon
March 1994   ISBN 0-88132-162-1

Reviving the European Union*
C. Randall Henning, Eduard Hochreiter, and Gary
Clyde Hufbauer, Editors
April 1994   ISBN 0-88132-208-3

China in the World Economy   Nicholas R. Lardy
April 1994   ISBN 0-88132-200-8

Greening the GATT: Trade, Environment, and the
Future   Daniel C. Esty
July 1994   ISBN 0-88132-205-9

Western Hemisphere Economic Integration
Gary Clyde Hufbauer and Jeffrey J. Schott
July 1994   ISBN 0-88132-159-1

Currencies and Politics in the United States,
Germany, and Japan
C. Randall Henning
September 1994   ISBN 0-88132-127-3

Estimating Equilibrium Exchange Rates
John Williamson, editor
September 1994   ISBN 0-88132-076-5

Managing the World Economy: Fifty Years After
Bretton Woods   Peter B. Kenen, editor
September 1994   ISBN 0-88132-212-1

Reciprocity and Retaliation in U.S. Trade Policy
Thomas O. Bayard and Kimberly Ann Elliott
September 1994   ISBN 0-88132-084-6

The Uruguay Round: An Assessment
Jeffrey J. Schott, assisted by Johanna W. Buurman
November 1994   ISBN 0-88132-206-7

Measuring the Costs of Protection in Japan
Yoko Sazanami, Shujiro Urata, and Hiroki Kawai
January 1995   ISBN 0-88132-211-3

Foreign Direct Investment in the United States,
3rd Ed.   Edward M. Graham and Paul R. Krugman
January 1995   ISBN 0-88132-204-0

The Political Economy of Korea-United States
Cooperation*
C. Fred Bergsten and Il SaKong, editors/*February
1995*   ISBN 0-88132-213-X

International Debt Reexamined   William R. Cline
February 1995   ISBN 0-88132-083-8

American Trade Politics, 3rd Ed.   I.M. Destler
April 1995   ISBN 0-88132-215-6

Managing Official Export Credits: The Quest for a
Global Regime*   John E. Ray
July 1995   ISBN 0-88132-207-5

Asia Pacific Fusion: Japan's Role in APEC*
Yoichi Funabashi
October 1995   ISBN 0-88132-224-5

Korea-United States Cooperation in the New
World Order*
C. Fred Bergsten and Il SaKong, editors
February 1996   ISBN 0-88132-226-1

Why Exports Really Matter! * ISBN 0-88132-221-0
Why Exports Matter More!*   ISBN 0-88132-229-6
J. David Richardson and Karin Rindal
July 1995; February 1996

Global Corporations and National Governments
Edward M. Graham
May 1996   ISBN 0-88132-111-7

Global Economic Leadership and the Group of
Seven   C. Fred Bergsten and C. Randall Henning
May 1996   ISBN 0-88132-218-0

The Trading System After the Uruguay Round
John Whalley and Colleen Hamilton
July 1996   ISBN 0-88132-131-1

Private Capital Flows to Emerging Markets After
the Mexican Crisis   Guillermo A. Calvo,
Morris Goldstein, and Eduard Hochreiter
September 1996   ISBN 0-88132-232-6

The Crawling Band as an Exchange Rate Regime:
Lessons from Chile, Colombia, and Israel
John Williamson
September 1996   ISBN 0-88132-231-8

Flying High: Liberalizing Civil Aviation in the
Asia Pacific
Gary Clyde Hufbauer and Christopher Findlay
November 1996   ISBN 0-88132-227-X

Measuring the Costs of Visible Protection in
Korea   Namdoo Kim
November 1996   ISBN 0-88132-236-9

The World Trading System: Challenges Ahead
Jeffrey J. Schott
December 1996   ISBN 0-88132-235-0

Has Globalization Gone Too Far?   Dani Rodrik
March 1997   ISBN cloth 0-88132-243-1

Korea-United States Economic Relationship
C. Fred Bergsten and Il SaKong, editors
March 1997   ISBN 0-88132-240-7

Summitry in the Americas: A Progress Report
Richard E. Feinberg
April 1997   ISBN 0-88132-242-3

Corruption and the Global Economy
Kimberly Ann Elliott
June 1997   ISBN 0-88132-233-4

Regional Trading Blocs in the World Economic
System   Jeffrey A. Frankel
October 1997   ISBN 0-88132-202-4

Sustaining the Asia Pacific Miracle: Environmental Protection and Economic Integration   André Dua and Daniel C. Esty
October 1997   ISBN 0-88132-250-4
Trade and Income Distribution   William R. Cline
November 1997   ISBN 0-88132-216-4
Global Competition Policy
Edward M. Graham and J. David Richardson
December 1997   ISBN 0-88132-166-4
Unfinished Business: Telecommunications after the Uruguay Round
Gary Clyde Hufbauer and Erika Wada
December 1997   ISBN 0-88132-257-1
Financial Services Liberalization in the WTO
Wendy Dobson and Pierre Jacquet
June 1998   ISBN 0-88132-254-7
Restoring Japan's Economic Growth
Adam S. Posen
September 1998   ISBN 0-88132-262-8
Measuring the Costs of Protection in China
Zhang Shuguang, Zhang Yansheng, and Wan Zhongxin
November 1998   ISBN 0-88132-247-4
Foreign Direct Investment and Development: The New Policy Agenda for Developing Countries and Economies in Transition
Theodore H. Moran
December 1998   ISBN 0-88132-258-X
Behind the Open Door: Foreign Enterprises in the Chinese Marketplace   Daniel H. Rosen
January 1999   ISBN 0-88132-263-6
Toward A New International Financial Architecture: A Practical Post-Asia Agenda
Barry Eichengreen
February 1999   ISBN 0-88132-270-9
Is the U.S. Trade Deficit Sustainable?
Catherine L. Mann/*September 1999*
ISBN 0-88132-265-2
Safeguarding Prosperity in a Global Financial System: The Future International Financial Architecture, Independent Task Force Report Sponsored by the Council on Foreign Relations
Morris Goldstein, Project Director
October 1999   ISBN 0-88132-287-3
Avoiding the Apocalypse: The Future of the Two Koreas   Marcus Noland
June 2000   ISBN 0-88132-278-4
Assessing Financial Vulnerability: An Early Warning System for Emerging Markets
Morris Goldstein, Graciela Kaminsky, and Carmen Reinhart
June 2000   ISBN 0-88132-237-7
Global Electronic Commerce: A Policy Primer
Catherine L. Mann, Sue E. Eckert, and Sarah Cleeland Knight
July 2000   ISBN 0-88132-274-1

The WTO after Seattle
Jeffrey J. Schott, editor
July 2000   ISBN 0-88132-290-3
Intellectual Property Rights in the Global Economy   Keith E. Maskus
August 2000   ISBN 0-88132-282-2
The Political Economy of the Asian Financial Crisis   Stephan Haggard
August 2000   ISBN 0-88132-283-0
Transforming Foreign Aid: United States Assistance in the 21st Century   Carol Lancaster
August 2000   ISBN 0-88132-291-1
Fighting the Wrong Enemy: Antiglobal Activists and Multinational Enterprises
Edward M. Graham
September 2000   ISBN 0-88132-272-5

SPECIAL REPORTS

1   Promoting World Recovery: A Statement on Global Economic Strategy*
     by Twenty-six Economists from Fourteen Countries
     December 1982   ISBN 0-88132-013-7
2   Prospects for Adjustment in Argentina, Brazil, and Mexico: Responding to the Debt Crisis*   John Williamson, editor
     June 1983   ISBN 0-88132-016-1
3   Inflation and Indexation: Argentina, Brazil, and Israel*   John Williamson, editor
     March 1985   ISBN 0-88132-037-4
4   Global Economic Imbalances*
     C. Fred Bergsten, editor
     March 1986   ISBN 0-88132-042-0
5   African Debt and Financing*
     Carol Lancaster and John Williamson, editors
     May 1986   ISBN 0-88132-044-7
6   Resolving the Global Economic Crisis: After Wall Street*
     Thirty-three Economists from Thirteen Countries
     December 1987   ISBN 0-88132-070-6
7   World Economic Problems
     Kimberly Ann Elliott and John Williamson, editors
     April 1988   ISBN 0-88132-055-2
     Reforming World Agricultural Trade*
     Twenty-nine Professionals from Seventeen Countries
     1988   ISBN 0-88132-088-9
8   Economic Relations Between the United States and Korea: Conflict or Cooperation?*
     Thomas O. Bayard and Soo-Gil Young, editors
     January 1989   ISBN 0-88132-068-4

WORKS IN PROGRESS

The Impact of Increased Trade on
Organized Labor in the United States
Robert E. Baldwin
New Regional Arrangements and the World
Economy
C. Fred Bergsten
The Globalization Backlash in Europe and the
United States
C. Fred Bergsten, Pierre Jacquet, and Karl Kaiser
The U.S.-Japan Economic Relationship
C. Fred Bergsten, Marcus Noland, and
Takatoshi Ito
China's Entry to the World Economy
Richard N. Cooper
World Capital Markets: Challenges to
the G-10
Wendy Dobson and Gary Clyde Hufbauer
The ILO in the World Economy
Kimberly Ann Elliott
Reforming Economic Sanctions
Kimberly Ann Elliott, Gary C. Hufbauer, and
Jeffrey J. Schott
Free Trade in Labor Agency Services
Kimberly Ann Elliott and J. David Richardson
The *Chaebol* and Structural Problems in Korea
Edward M. Graham

NAFTA: A Seven Year Appraisal of the Trade,
Environment, and Labor Agreements
Gary Clyde Hufbauer and Jeffrey J. Schott
Ex-Im Bank in the 21st Century
Gary Clyde Hufbauer and Rita Rodriquez, eds.
Prospects for Western Hemisphere Free Trade
Gary Clyde Hufbauer and Jeffrey J. Schott
Price Integration in the World Economy
Gary Clyde Hufbauer, Erika Wada, and
Tony Warren
Reforming the IMF
Peter Kenen
Imports, Exports, and American Industrial
Workers since 1979
Lori G. Kletzer
Reemployment Experiences of Trade-
Displaced Americans
Lori G. Kletzer
Globalization and Creative Destruction in the
US Textile and Apparel Industry
James Levinsohn
Measuring the Costs of Protection in Europe
Patrick Messerlin
Dollarization, Currency Blocs, and U.S. Policy
Adams S. Posen
Germany in the World Economy after the
EMU
Adam S. Posen
Japan's Financial Crisis and Its Parallels to
U.S. Experience
Adam S. Posen and Ryoichi Mikitani, eds.
Sizing Up Globalization: The Globalization
Balance Sheet Capstone Volume
J. David Richardson
Why Global Integration Matters Most!
J. David Richardson and Howard Lewis
Worker Perceptions and Pressures in the
Global Economy
Matthew J. Slaughter
India in the World Economy
T. N. Srinivasan and Suresh D. Tendulka

Australia, New Zealand, and Papua New Guinea
D.A. INFORMATION SERVICES
648 Whitehorse Road
Mitcham, Victoria 3132, Australia
tel: 61-3-9210-7777
fax: 61-3-9210-7788
e-mail: service@dadirect.com.au
http://www.dadirect.com.au

Caribbean
SYSTEMATICS STUDIES LIMITED
St. Augustine Shopping Centre
Eastern Main Road, St. Augustine
Trinidad and Tobago, West Indies
tel: 868-645-8466
fax: 868-645-8467
e-mail: tobe@trinidad.net

United Kingdom and Europe (including Russia and Turkey)
The Eurospan Group
3 Henrietta Street, Covent Garden
London WC2E 8LU England
tel: 44-20-7240-0856
fax: 44-20-7379-0609
http://www.eurospan.co.uk

Northern Africa and the Middle East (Egypt, Algeria, Bahrain, Palestine, Jordan, Kuwait, Lebanon, Libya, Morocco, Oman, Qatar, Saudi Arabia, Syria, Tunisia, Yemen, and United Arab Emirates)
Middle East Readers Information Center (MERIC)
2 bahgat Aly Street
El-Masry Towers, Tower #D, Apt. #24, First Floor
Zamalek, Cairo EGYPT
tel: 202-341-3824/340 3818;
fax 202-341-9355
http://www.meric-co.com

Taiwan
Unifacmanu Trading Co., Ltd.
4F, No. 91, Ho-Ping East Rd, Sect. 1
Taipei 10609, Taiwan
tel: 886-2-23419646
fax: 886-2-23943103
e-mail: winjoin@ms12.hinet.net

Argentina
World Publications SA.
Av. Cordoba 1877
1120 Buenos Aires, Argentina
tel/fax: (54 11) 4815 8156
e-mail:
http://wpbooks@infovia.com.ar

People's Republic of China (including Hong Kong) **and Taiwan** (sales representatives):
Tom Cassidy
Cassidy & Associates
70 Battery Place, Ste 220
New York, NY 10280
tel: 212-706-2200   fax: 212-706-2254
e-mail: CHINACAS@Prodigy.net

India, Bangladesh, Nepal, and Sri Lanka
Viva Books Pvt.
Mr. Vinod Vasishtha
4325/3, Ansari Rd.
Daryaganj, New Delhi-110002
INDIA
tel: 91-11-327-9280
fax: 91-11-326-7224 ,
e-mail: vinod.viva@gndel.globalnet.
ems.vsnl.net.in

South Africa
Pat Bennink
Dryad Books
PO Box 11684
Vorna Valley 1686
South Africa
tel: +27 14 576 1332
fax: +27 82 899 9156
e-mail: dryad@hixnet.co.za

Thailand
Asia Books 5 Sukhumvit Rd. Soi 61
Bangkok 10110 Thailand
(phone 662-714-0740-2 Ext: 221, 222, 223
fax: (662) 391-2277)
e-mail: purchase@asiabooks.co.th
http://www.asiabooksonline.com

Canada
RENOUF BOOKSTORE
5369 Canotek Road, Unit 1,
Ottawa, Ontario K1J 9J3, Canada
tel: 613-745-2665
fax: 613-745-7660
http://www.renoufbooks.com

Colombia, Ecuador, and Peru
Infoenlace Ltda
Attn: Octavio Rojas
Calle 72 No. 13-23 Piso 3
Edificio Nueva Granada, Bogota, D.C.
Colombia
tel: (571) 255 8783 or 255 7969
fax: (571) 248 0808 or 217 6435

Japan and the Republic of Korea
United Publishers Services, Ltd.·
Kenkyu-Sha Bldg.
9, Kanda Surugadai 2-Chome
Chiyoda-Ku, Tokyo 101
JAPAN
tel: 81-3-3291-4541;
fax: 81-3-3292-8610
e-mail: saito@ups.co.jp
For trade accounts only.
Individuals will find IIE books in leading Tokyo bookstores.

South America
Julio E. Emod
Publishers Marketing & Research
Associates, c/o HARBRA
Rua Joaquim Tavora, 629
04015-001 Sao Paulo, Brasil
tel: (55) 11-571-1122;
fax: (55) 11-575-6876
e-mail: emod@harbra.com.br

**Visit our Web site at:
http://www.iie.com
E-mail orders to:
orders@iie.com**